KANSAS SCHOOL OF RELIGION
University of Kansas
1300 Oread Avenue
LAWRENCE, KANSAS 66044

By Gibson Winter

LOVE AND CONFLICT
THE SUBURBAN CAPTIVITY OF THE CHURCHES
NEW CREATION AS METROPOLIS
ELEMENTS FOR A SOCIAL ETHIC

Religious Identity

STUDIES IN RELIGION AND SOCIETY SERIES

Religious Identity

A STUDY OF
RELIGIOUS ORGANIZATION

by Gibson Winter

The Macmillan Company, New York
Collier-Macmillan Ltd., London

First Printing
THE MACMILLAN COMPANY, NEW YORK
COLLIER-MACMILLAN CANADA LTD., TORONTO, ONTARIO

Printed in the United States of America

Portions of this book were previously published under the title
"Religious Organizations" in *The Emergent American Society*
edited by W. Lloyd Warner, Copyright © 1967 by Yale University.

1. Religious and ecclesiastical institutions
   — United States
2. Institutionalism (Religion)
3. United States — Religion.

CONTENTS

Preface

This study was originally proposed by W. Lloyd Warner as an aspect of his research on large-scale organization in American society. The author, with students and colleagues, working in the Center for the Scientific Study of Religion in the early 1960's before that organization had achieved formal status, carried out an exploratory research in the field of religious organization. That material was finally published in the first volume of Mr. Warner's study *The Emergent American Society*. With Lloyd Warner's permission, the author has made a thorough revision and updating of the study for more general circulation. This is the first of a series of studies in Religion and Society which are being produced in the Center.

It is evident from this study that much work needs to be done on large-scale religious organization. The present study is the only major step beyond the pioneering work of Paul Harrison in his volume *Authority and Power in the Free Church Tradition*. The present study carries the analysis up to the detailed inquiries on informal organization of power. Such studies become more possible within the broader framework which the present study develops. This volume is, then, a contribution to a developing field of research. The appendix on "Needs for Further Research" formulates some of the areas for exploration which have been located in this inquiry.

Reference occurs in the footnotes to particular contributions of different men to this study. However, mention should be made here of the work of John Paynter on the organization of the Disciples of Christ and the Methodist Church; Robert Benne on three major synods of the Lutheran Church, Robert Bates on the history of mass evangelism and the organization of the Billy Graham campaigns, much of which could not be incorporated in this study for lack of space; Stanley Hallett on the Church Federation of Greater Chicago; Michael Schiltz on the objective data available on Catholic organization; and many fine studies done by Jewish scientists on the emergence of Jewish organization in the United States.

In addition to specific investigations, the author is indebted to Paul Mundy, Rabbi Robert J. Marx, Abbott Rosen, Robert Nelson, a representative of the National Council of Catholic Bishops, and especially to Widick Schroeder for advice and criticism on the manuscript. The footnotes attest to the enormous quantity of scholarly work which was done by others without which this overview of large-scale religious organization would not have been possible.

A special word of appreciation is due to Cynthia

Donnelly who has assumed responsibility for editing the Studies in Religion and Society so that they may become readable documents in the common language. The major difficulty with scientific research on society, especially where it overlaps with other disciplines such as theology, is that it becomes the hidden preserve of a smaller and smaller group of scholars. These studies are concerned with matters of importance to broad sectors of our community. Mrs. Donnelly's work is an important step in making them accessible to this community.

GIBSON WINTER

Religious Identity

One

EXPANSION OR REVOLUTION

Religious Organization in the New Society

Religion has emerged in the United States as a major organizational enterprise, although its scope and complexity may seem rather insignificant in comparison with industrial and governmental organizations. The numerical change in religious membership gives some hint of this organizational revolution. In 1890 the membership of the twenty principal religious bodies represented 94 percent of the country's religious membership; these twenty bodies organized the activities of 20.5 million members. In addition to these major bodies there were 533 congregations of Jewish affiliation and 123 other small religious groups. The membership of the twenty principal bodies of 1960 represented 88 percent of the nation's religious membership; these twenty bodies organized the religious activities of 114 million members. At that time there were also 4,079 congregations of Jewish affiliation and 239 small religious groups.[1]

To speak of religious organization over this seventy-year period is at least to reckon with a membership explosion of major proportions, correlated, to be sure, with growth of population. In this same period there has been a shift from a rural to an increasingly urban constituency. Expansion and change characterize this period of religious life in the United States, whether one investigates membership, expenditure for buildings, missions, benevolence, federation, or merger.[2]

The expansion in religious organization and activities is only one aspect of an extremely complex transformation in the internal life of the major faiths and their external relationships to the larger American community. It is for this reason that we are led to speak of a revolution rather than an expansion in scale of religious organization. One aspect of this fundamental transformation is undoubtedly the change occurring in the organization of American society. A brief consideration of the character of this change may set the stage for our examination of the internal changes which have occurred in the major religious bodies.

It has become commonplace to speak of the emer-

[1] Sources for these comparisons are the United States Census, 1890; Statistics of the Churches, p. xxiv, and The Yearbook of American Churches, 1960; no brief is held for the accuracy of religious statistics, which are notoriously unstable, but the comparison is not out of line with specific observations.

[2] An analysis of the transformations in membership from 1870 to 1950 is given in the author's book, The Suburban Captivity of the Churches (New York, Doubleday & Company, Inc., 1960).

gence of an organizational society in which control of activities becomes centered in large, bureaucratic structures. If there were any doubt about this phenomenon, W. Lloyd Warner's recent volume, *The Emergent American Society*, furnishes more than sufficient confirmation of this extensive organizational development,[3] and recognition that this book recognizes that more and more sectors of our experience are organized by rationalized processes, subjected to a hierarchical principle of subordination, and integrated across extensive areas encompassing a multiplicity of activities. When one considers, for example, the highly controlled process of an automobile industry and the complex set of activities over national and global areas which it integrates, the notion of large-scale organization gains some concreteness. However, it is only during a strike or similar crisis that one becomes at all aware of this complex network which is maintained as a flow of information and control along vertical and horizontal lines. The intensity of communicative exchanges, the rapidity of movement and the extensiveness of impact of such massive organization is one aspect of the emergence of a society of large-scale organizations. This aspect could be summarized under the notion of *scale*. One aspect of transformation in the past century is change in scale of the first magnitude.

Another aspect is increasing complexity of the societal processes, generated by the differentiation in spheres and sectors of activities. Young people experience this complexity in an existential way as they confront the perplexing problems of vocation. To be

[3] W. Lloyd Warner, D. B. Unawalla, and J. H. Trimm, *The Emergent American Society* (New Haven and London: Yale University Press).

sure, there are many young people in the under-classed areas of the cities and in the backwaters of rural poverty who may never have an opportunity to contribute to the society, since one aspect of this complexity is to conceal those whom the machine rejects. However, those who gain access to an education find it increasingly difficult to determine the course they wish to follow, since the diversification of possible specializations, even within a particular field, continues to mount. Complexity is also experienced in the segregation of various sectors of experience, where family and residence become the locus of a community which may be quite radically separated from community of work, and for some people from community of friends or religious community. We are members of a congeries of communities, in each of which we have certain commitments and gain certain rewards, but in none of which we may feel truly at home or ourselves. Divisions between public and private sectors, insulation of one structure or interest from another, become commonplace. The critical problem of complexity in a highly technical society may well become the lack of unifying or overarching symbols which maintain a sense of common life. We shall come back to this problem in considering the struggle of the religious bodies to maintain their relationships with these various structures. In this introductory note, it is sufficient to recognize that the organizational revolution has not only confronted the religious bodies with problems of scale but also with the need for *diversification of activities* and agencies.

A third aspect of the organizational revolution is the phenomenon of secularization which has become increasingly important during the last century of

American life. Secularization is the reference of various cultural and societal processes to principles immanent to their own nature rather than to transcendent principles of authority. The whole American experience has been one of increasing secularization, beginning with several colonies under established religious control, proceeding to separation of church and state, and gradually moving toward an independence of cultural institutions and morality from the direct interventions of religious authoritiy. To be sure, some educational institutions, some codes of morality in various states, and some practices of censorship are still sponsored and controlled by religious agencies, but secularity no longer carries any presumption of moral or spiritual wrong. In fact, some major religious thinkers of recent years have taken the term secular upon themselves and affirmed that this is more than the condition of a few in the contemporary world. However one perceives the problem of secularity, *increasing secularization of life* has freed many sectors for antonomous development and presented the religious bodies with new problems of mission and ministry.

The traditional pattern of American religious life had been to concentrate on the cultivation of spiritual life in the congregation, parish, or synagogue, thus indirectly leavening and molding the life of the nation. Religious groups occasionally broke out of this pattern in mass campaigns of evangelism and mass attacks on common problems such as slavery or alcohol. In general, nevertheless, the religious agencies worked through the private sector on behalf of the public good. This whole strategy has gradually been coming into question with the organizational differentiation of the society and the secularizing of various sectors of life. These are the kinds of problems which have confronted the religious bodies in the course of their organizational revolution. It is no longer enough to set up denominational colleges to guide the young. These colleges are all but disengaged from the religious heritage. The young people in turn participate in a culture quite alien to the traditional teachings of the denomination.

This review of three aspects of organizational transformation—scale, complexity and secularity—sets the stage for considering some basic problems with which these bodies have had to contend, furnishing us with some dimensions to consider as we examine the course of the revolution in religious organization.

THE PROBLEMS OF RELIGIOUS ORGANIZATION

A crucial problem of any organization is the principle of order or authority that informs it. This is a critical problem in religious organization, especially in a society which established a voluntary principle of religious membership after the federal union was achieved. The voluntary principle, as we shall see, set a dynamic at work which has been pervasive in religious organization in the American experience. However, the three major faiths—Protestant, Catholic and Jewish—also operated with specific principles of order. These principles issue from the fundamental religious visions which have informed these faiths and the grounds on which their communities have been constituted. Hence, the common principle of voluntary membership is radically modified by the distinctive principles of order out of which the various major communions have lived.

A religious community has the problem of its own internal continuity as a community of faith. This requires some ordering principle which can define the scope of ideological and organizational activities which legitimately fall within its organization. Furthermore, the control of instrumentalities through which the faith-community maintains its relationships to the larger society requires a principle of order. However, that principle has to be flexible enough to free agencies for interchange with a rapidly changing society for which there are few precedents or guidelines. Moreover, problems of control and flexibility have to be solved whether the religious body is preoccupied with missionary extension or with maintaining its own integrity and identity within a larger community.

A second problem of organization is the extent and quality of participation or representation which it achieves: the one-way or two-way exchange of information and interests effected within the organizational network. The problem of participation becomes increasingly acute as the scale of organizational development grows. Paul Harrison investigated this problem in the presumably democratic American Baptist Convention, where the development of a staff of experts on a national level eventuated in informal control over policy by experts. This problem may be aggravated in a religious body which has no theological ground for authority in such a massive organization—the Baptist case—but it is also an almost inevitable concomitant of the scale of such organizations and the managerial expertise required. However, representative processes can be instituted and enhanced through better techniques of communication, but this calls for clearer theology and conscious design of participatory processes. In any case, accountability of staff and responsibility of membership forms a second major problem confronting large-scale religious organizations.

A third problem is the relevance of religious faiths within the larger society. We have already considered an aspect of this problem under the rubric of secularization. However, the problem is more general. It pertains to any organization which either lives by exchanges with the society, as in the case of an educational or productive organization, or furnishes a fundamental motivation and global vision to the total society, as in the case of religious bodies. Relevance has become an important term in religious vocabulary in recent decades, perhaps in large part because of the increasing sense of isolation which religious groups have felt. A basic tension is at least discernible now in the three major faiths between a preoccupation of religious organization with survival and concern for the social and cultural impact of the organization. There is undoubtedly much common ground between the concerns, and the tendency to polarization may be a very transitory phenomenon. Nevertheless, the growing crises in urban life have provoked some radical concern for relevance in all three faith-communities, and set up some deep tensions within those more concerned for the maintenance and growth of the internal strength of the organizations. Both groups may be concerned for the well-being of the faith-community and the society, but their vision of public responsibility is radically different.

From our perspective on the broad problems of religious organization, we have to recognize that relevance without organization will effect little, and strong organization which is irrelevant may not be worth much. Survival and relevance are two inseparable aspects of religious identity. The revolution in organization has attempted to keep both elements in some kind of harmony.

It seems dramatic to speak of revolution in considering the changes through which religious organization has passed in the last century in the United States. It is certainly not true that the fundamental values and guiding principles of authority in these faith-communities have been overthrown. There are permanent elements in these structures which make it possible to identify and trace the changes through which they have passed. However, our national life has undergone nothing less than a revolution in its movement from an agrarian and early industrial period to the large-scale organization of a complex, highly technical society. This is a different world on many levels of experience, and the religious communities have participated in that transformation. The revolution in religious organization has come, in fact, more on the level of organization than in fundamental vision and order. This may have been a source of strain, as we shall observe, but it has also been the source of power and continuity in these religious organizations. The revolution was a necessity, if our reading of the societal situation is at all accurate. It may well be that the revolution has not gone far enough or still has many turns to go before an adequate structure is achieved. Whatever the final judgment on this issue, the organizational revolution has been fundamental and far-reaching in significance, shaping the religious identities of the major faiths.

THE SCOPE OF THE STUDY

We shall attempt to describe and document that revolution, identifying the common elements in Protestant, Catholic, and Jewish developments, while giving due recognition to differences. That there would be common elements could perhaps be predicted from the general acceptance in American religious life of what Sidney Mead has called the voluntary principle: that is, the use of special associations and agencies—task forces, voluntary associations, boards and committees—to cope with emerging problems. Originally described by Mead because of its importance in American Christianity, this principle has been equally characteristic of the Jewish congregations, and for that matter of American social and political movements as well.[4] The voluntary principle achieved expression in religious life under and in spite of various restraints. Some religious communities, such as the Roman Catholic, demanded orthodoxy in hierarchical and institutional forms as well as in forms of worship. To a greater or lesser degree, however, the voluntary principle did influence all of these institutions, just as the emerging social and cultural situation set them common problems.

The result for religious organizations was the development of the agency and its attendant organization. We shall have occasion to examine this process in some detail. The proliferation of agencies posed a serious problem of unity of command within the religious organizations, for agencies grew up before a corresponding ideology or ecclesiology was developed

[4] Sidney E. Mead, "Denominationalism: The Shape of Protestantism in America," in *Church History*, 23 (1954) 291–320.

for their control. It is not surprising, in terms of Daniel Boorstin's interpretation of American political development, that an organizational problem of such a simple, everyday character should arise, although it is somewhat unexpected in the religious field, in which careful appeal to, and elaboration of, doctrine is normally regarded as crucial.[5]

The theological problem of organizations goes back to the beginnings of Christianity, and for the Jewish community to the Old Testament. The difficulty of coming to terms with organizational elaboration is much greater for such American bodies as the American Baptist Convention and the Disciples of Christ, which anchor their organizational position in the primitive, relatively undeveloped stage of church organization, than it is, for instance, for the Episcopal Church, the Presbyterian Church, the Lutheran bodies, or the Roman Catholic Church, all of which provide for some type of development in ecclesiastical structure.

Several consequences followed from these ambiguities in ecclesiological formulation:

1. The problem of church unity of command was aggravated by differing perspectives on the validity of given forms of organization, particularly when the mergers of denominations brought together conflicting traditions of organization.

2. The goals of an organized activity could easily become divorced from the organization's original theological task because there was no clear articulation of the task's relationship to the administrative form used to achieve it.

3. The parent religious organization was often

[5] Daniel Boorstin, *The Genius of American Politics* (Chicago, University of Chicago Press, 1958), especially Chapter I.

denied effective participation in the decision-making of an agency as a result of the church's failure to become organizationally sophisticated.

Such problems, underlying themes in the history of religious institutions, become much more pressing in a period of organizational revolution.

The term *organized* is usually applied to churches in a pejorative way, particularly with reference to activities peripheral to "religious" matters. This fact calls for some clarification. Organization is the application of rational processes of coordination and communication to achieve clearly defined goals or objectives. In this sense almost any human activity is amenable to some degree of organization; in fact, one way we distinguish the commonsense world of everyday life from dreaming, fantasy, and aesthetic enjoyment is by the degree of organization expected in our activities and responses. We do not expect dreams to manifest their contents in highly organized forms. Many dreams seem to reorder haphazardly the basic themes of everyday life. Organization means a rational ordering of various elements and phases directed toward the effective realization of an anticipated state of affairs.[6]

This is the meaning of the term organization as we apply it to the various religious faiths: primarily the coordination of activities, the introduction of rational systems of accounting, the use of functionally specialized staffs, the application of objective criteria to gauge performance, and the designation of specific goals to be served by functional units within the

[6] Alfred Schutz, *Collected Papers, Vol. I: The Problem of Social Reality* (The Hague, Martinus Nijhoff, 1962), especially the essay "On Multiple Realities."

enterprise. Our principal task will be to give an account of the extent and character of elaboration of organization within the religious bodies, and then to consider the functional problems arising from this elaboration, and the direction in which resolution of these problems is being sought.

Because of the vast organizational development in a short compass, and the limited research available, one can only hope to establish profiles of these religious organizations at this time. The complex problems of informal organization require investigation of the "hard" data of interpersonal communications in these organizations, and only a limited amount of such data is available.

Paul Harrison's study of the American Baptist Convention blazed the way for the study of religious organization in the Protestant tradition.[7] Without his study this essay would not have been possible, not only because his research uncovered some very important data, but also because the major lines of organizational development were already evident in it. It is a basic study of a Protestant denomination— the American Baptist Convention—whose theological understanding anchors religious authority in the individual believer, or at most in a congregation of believers.

We have established a study parallel to Harrison's in an examination of the historical records of the organizational development and elaboration of the Disciples of Christ, whose ecclesiology is somewhat

[7] Paul M. Harrison, *Authority and Power in the Free Church Tradition* (Princeton, Princeton University Press, 1959); in addition, many historical texts contributed substantially to the data and theory.

comparable. Complementary to these is the study of Methodist organization, done to contrast a much larger denomination developed from a preachers' church governed by the ordained.[8] In contrast to the two studies of lay Christianity (Baptist and Disciples) and the study of the preachers' church (Methodism), an examination of the organizational development of three Lutheran denominations on a regional level provides some picture of organizations in more confessional and liturgical traditions.[9] We have also available the work of Valorous Clear, who carried out research on the transition of the Church of God from an informal structure to a formal organization.[10] This careful study provides illuminating insight into the dynamics of the organization's process because it concentrates in a short time a process that took many years in the more formal denominations.

In addition to these denominations, we have investigated a federation of churches in a major metropolitan area. This distinctively Protestant form of religious organization mirrors the major lines of denomination organization, since a council or federation manifests the coordinated organizational thrusts

[8] The studies of the Disciples of Christ and the Methodist Church were done in collaboration with John Paynter; this research would not have been possible without his thorough investigation of these denominations. These were historical investigations of journals and records, later checked with several authorities in the Methodist tradition to verify interpretations.

[9] The Lutheran studies were done in collaboration with Robert Benne; his creative approach to this research contributed data and theoretical formulation to the total project. This study included a review of records and interviews with the regional executives of the three major Lutheran bodies including interviews of executives.

[10] Valorous Clear, "The Church of God: A Study in Social Adaptation," Dissertation in Partial Fulfillment of Requirement for Ph.D., University of Chicago, 1953, unpublished.

of various religious groups.[11] Here too some "hard"
data were available for consultation and reference;
they provided extremely interesting clues to the problems of the denominations, because an organizational
study of the National Council of the Churches of
Christ in America, recently completed, was of great
importance in discerning trends.[12]

Finally, a study was made of the pattern of organization of the evangelistic movements, as represented
by Billy Sunday and Billy Graham.[13]

Sufficient data are thus available for drawing an
initial profile of the organizational revolution in Protestantism. The adequacy of the data will be indicated at each stage in the presentation. Although
there is no question that much further research is
needed, and generalizations about the Protestant profile have to be made with reservations, the general
picture is reasonably clear. The most serious gap in

[11] Research on the Church Federation of Greater Chicago was
contributed by Stanley Hallett and helped to broaden the perspective on the denominational development; the author is also
indebted to Mr. Hallett for his contributions of theory. This
study was done from the inside including a study of records and
examination of personnel and policies and discussion with staff.

[12] The study of the National Council of Churches of Christ
in the U.S.A. is being carried through by Booz, Allen and Hamilton, Management Consultants; this is a confidential study, as
indicated, but the problems and insights in the study were illuminating on the total spectrum of Protestant development.
The basic insights of this study were borne out by our own
research on a regional level.

[13] This investigation was made by Robert Bates, and, although
much of the data could not be incorporated into this volume,
the larger perspective on religious organization was strengthened
by the research; revivalism, as Sidney Mead has noted, is one of
the distinguishing marks of Protestantism in the United States
and no study of organization can afford to omit it. In addition
to historical study, an interview study of the Billy Graham Chicago Crusade—35 counselors and participants—shed light on
organizational aspects of revivalism.

this presentation of Protestantism is the omission of the pattern of organization in the Negro Protestant churches.[14] In addition, a study of the Presbyterian organization and the more hierarchial pattern of the Episcopal structure would serve to balance out our picture of Protestant development.

Generalizations about the profile of such a complex phenomenon as American Judaism could not be attempted without the excellent studies by Marshall Sklare, Nathan Glazer, Robert MacIver, and many others.[15] MacIver's study of the Jewish Community Relations Agencies is most illuminating, although it provoked considerable controversy at the time of its submission. This controversy disclosed some of the trends in Jewish organization, trends which have significant counterparts in Protestantism. Such comparisons need to be made with reserve; however, it is easy to overlook the commonalities in the emerging pattern of American society, and we need to strike some kind of balance between a proper concern for differences and an honest acknowledgement of the common patterns of organization that have arisen in response to very similar problems.

In some ways our picture of the Roman Catholic

[14] The Protestant denominations have approached such homogeneity that Gerhard Lenski found it difficult to discriminate among them with reference to the many variables he had explored; on the other hand, Negro Protestants showed up in the Detroit Area data as markedly different from white Protestants on many points. See Gerhard Lenski, *The Religious Factor* (Garden City, N.Y., Doubleday, 1961); J. R. Washington, Jr., *Black Religion* (Boston, Beacon Printers, 1964); and the author's discussion in *The Suburban Captivity of the Churches*.

[15] For references to these works, see the text. The author is especially indebted to Abbott Rosen of the Anti-Defamation League of B'nai B'rith for access to the MacIver Report and for counsel on the Jewish profile; needless to say, Mr. Rosen is in no way responsible for any opinions expressed in this volume.

organization is most adequate and clearcut.[16] The Roman Catholic faith manifests itself through a much more clearly defined institutional structure than the other faiths on the American scene. To this extent the lines of its organizational patterning are more definite; in fact, those lines are rather precisely specified in Canon Law. However, organizational development has also come about through voluntary associations, linked to the hierarchy and yet somewhat free to pursue their functional tasks. We have investigated the organizational growth of Catholic administration and voluntary agencies. A profile of Catholic organizational development emerges when these investigations are set against some of the historical studies by Catholic authors. However, we need much more internal data on the development of power between administrative and parochial units, on the adequacy of the overloaded diocesan machinery in the huge urban areas, on the allocation of resources in a rapidly changing metropolis, and, perhaps more importantly, on the informal exercise of influence between voluntary associations and hierarchical authorities. Such internal information will be difficult to obtain, partly because it may impinge on the traditional authority of the bishop. Nevertheless, such information is needed for an adequate profile of the direction in which Catholic organization is moving, and would be of great importance to the heirarchy of American Catholicism. Meanwhile, we can make certain general statements about the lines of

[16] Research by Michael Schiltz made possible the analysis of Roman Catholic organization; the author is deeply indebted to Mr. Schiltz for the clarity of his understanding of the emerging organizational problems in this vast, religious structure; this research was based on existing records in the religious body and some of the extant fine historical studies.

force which seem to be emerging; these statements, made with reserve, may prove fruitful in suggesting significant directions for further research.

The justification for drawing profiles of religious organization at this stage in research is that we have enough data to see our way. A profile is not a detail map, nor is it a dynamic analysis of operative forces in their consistent patterning. Profiles yield guidelines for evaluating problems and possibilities in organizational development. They cannot do more. We therefore set about the task of sketching these configurations without any illusion that more is possible at the present time.

Two

PROTESTANT DEVELOPMENT

The phenomenon of organizational growth can be measured by growth of administrative staff relative to local units and by centralized expenditure relative to budgeting for local needs. These indices convey some measure of degree of centralization. The first step in shaping a profile of Protestant organization is to assess the degree of administrative centralization that has occurred. We consider this process first in the Disciples of Christ and the Methodist Church.

GROWTH OF ADMINISTRATIVE STAFF

The Disciples of Christ, formed in the mid-nineteenth century, under the leadership of Alexander Campbell, was one of the movements for restoration of New Testament Christianity. It created a "General Convention of the Christian Churches of the United States of America" in 1849,[17] although prior to this meeting societies of individuals and congregations had gathered in various regions. Even the apparently formal meeting of 1849 represented a body whose principle of organization was primarily individual, at most congregational. Missionary societies formed within the community of Disciples as voluntary associations, but throughout the latter half of the 19th century tensions existed over the assimilation of such boards to a certified body. The basic problems confronting home and foreign mission boards involved regularizing collections from congregations rather than operating on individual subscriptions. Since by 1892 some regularized collections had been established, this date gives a baseline for estimating changes in administrative staff.

Although formal support for development of full-time, paid Disciples staff was delayed until revision of the constitution in 1939, staff developed through the earlier period; the gradual growth of social welfare activities, Bible School department, and missions activity led to increasing centralization of program. The figures in Table I (Appendix) reflect a proc-

[17] General historical information on the Disciples of Christ is drawn from W. E. Garrison and A. T. DeGroot, *The Disciples of Christ, A History* (St. Louis, Christian Board of Publication, 1948); Yearbook data for the Disciples will be classified as *Yearbook* for the appropriate year, although the yearbooks follow different nomenclature and sponsorship in different periods; 1892 and 1895, Christian Publishing Company; *American Home Missionary*, Yearbook issue for 1897, 1903–1918; American Christian Missionary Society, 1920; the United Christian Missionary Society, 1921–35; Yearbook Publication Committee, 1936–46; International Convention of Disciples of Christ, 1947–62. (Data on charts and for tables will simply be listed as *Yearbook* for convenience, but reference should be made to the proper publication for a particular year.)

ess of urbanization in recent decades, and consequently an increasing size of congregation, accounting in part for the gradual growth in membership and decline in number of churches from the peak year of 1908. The significant figures for centralization, however, are the proportionate increase in administrative staff relative to non-national ministry (those not on national agencies) and to churches since 1940. These are the decades of formalization in the denomination and are marked by a doubling in central staff, from 68 to 162, without appreciable increase in membership. In fact, the central staff increase by ten times since 1900 is in sharp contrast to the increase in membership over the same period by little more than half.

Before considering comparable figures for administrative development in Methodism, it may be helpful to indicate the rather complex process of Methodist development.[18] The "Christmas Conference" of Methodists in 1784 is usually taken as the date of establishment of the Methodist Episcopal Church as an independent body, although Methodist preachers had been meeting annually in America since 1773. From this starting point two lines of

[18] Several secondary sources provide information on the historical development of Methodism in the United States; R. W. Goodloe, "The Office of Bishop in the Methodist Church," Ph.D. Dissertation, University of Chicago, 1929, unpublished; N. B. Harmon, *The Organization of the Methodist Church* (New York, Abingdon-Cokesbury Press, 1948); J. L. Peters, *Christian Perfection and American Methodism* (New York, Abingdon Press, 1956); W. W. Sweet, *Methodism in American History* (New York, The Methodist Book Concern, 1933). This study was completed prior to the merger of the Methodist Church and the Evangelical United Brethren to form The United Methodist Church—a merger which demonstrates the movement towards ever-increasing organizational growth.

organizational development concern us: (1) development of subgeneral or subnational units of organization below this General Conference level; (2) the formation of task-oriented boards or agencies.

Initially the bishops, elders (preachers set aside for supervisory work), and preachers formed the Conference and administrative structure. By 1792 the elders had become presiding elders (called district superintendents) and by 1820 were responsible for the quarterly conference (meeting of the circuit-unit) and the district conference. Thus the General Conference and lower-level quarterly and district conferences were operative in the early period of the westward expansion. Several other administrative units were necessary between these levels, since territories were vast in this period and opportunities for coordination essential. The Annual Conference was established in 1792 as the basic administrative unit of Methodism, although the General Conference retained legislative responsibility and met quadrennially. The Annual Conference elected delegates who in turn comprised the legislative body of the General Conference. Certainly by the 1870's, the Annual Conference and its Board structures had become pivotal in the administration of Methodist activities. The Board, commission, and committee structures that were developing in Methodism during the nineteenth century were later reproduced on the district conference level so that an extensive administrative machinery was being elaborated on each of these conference levels.

The episcopal areas developed simultaneously, since bishops originally traveled throughout the entire Methodist community and were only gradually urged to define particular territories of responsibility. By 1872 the General Conference expressed its desire for stable residence of bishops by areas, and by 1924 this definition of responsibility was clarified. The bishops developed principal organizational ties to the Annual Conference, and with the merger in 1939 of the Methodist Episcopal, the Methodist Episcopal South, and the Methodist Protestant Churches, six jurisdictional conferences were established with meetings set quadrennially.[19] This complex picture of

[19] The Methodist Church was constituted in 1939 by the merger of the Methodist Episcopal, the Methodist Episcopal, South, and the Methodist Protestant Churches. In order to get a full view of the Methodist Church, one would need to examine each of its constituent strands. Such an approach has not been employed here primarily because of the unavailability of sources on the Methodist Episcopal, South, and the Methodist Protestant Churches. The General Conference Journals of the former were available but contain no systematic or thorough presentation of reports on the various General agencies. The Annual Conference minutes of the Church, South, were also available and the relevant statistics from that source are included. No primary sources whatsoever were available on the Methodist Protestant Church.

In the face of these handicaps only one alternative remained: to examine the development of the Methodist Episcopal Church up to the time of the merger and then to concentrate on the Methodist Church since 1939. This "last resort" is not, however, without internal justification. Quantitatively, the Methodist Episcopal Church constituted the largest of the three uniting bodies. In 1932 it recorded 3,908,262 members, 12,699 effective preachers, and 24,801 churches. The Methodist Episcopal Church, South, recorded 2,645,142 members, 6,610 effective preachers, 16,188 churches. The Methodist Protestant Church, according to the 1936 U.S. Census of Religious Bodies, recorded 148,288 members and 1,498 churches (no ministerial figures available).

Even more important than this quantitative consideration, however, is the high degree of continuity between the modes of organization in the Methodist Episcopal Church and the modes of organization in the Methodist Church. Not surprisingly, the largest of the three churches seems to have played the dominant role in the determination of the shape of the new church. This

conference levels and episcopal areas can be seen schematically in Chart I (Appendix) as two lines of administrative responsibility interconnected at crucial points: the episcopacy links to the General Conference with its commissions and committees, to the jurisdictional conference at the second level, and to the Annual Conference; the episcopacy is also related through the Board of Managers to the board structure, which is reproduced at each level; moreover, the district conference and quarterly conference levels operate under episcopal direction though not under direct supervision.

---

fact is the more understandable when it is realized that the Methodist Episcopal Church, South, according to both Sweet and Goodloe, followed a pattern of development very similar to that in the Methodist Episcopal Church.

The following sources were used to compile the charts and tables on Methodist organization; reference will be made simply to the Minutes of the Annual Conference or the Discipline or the Journal, but according to the year and the branch of Methodism, the actual publication can be checked.

The Methodist Yearbook
(1869–1933)   The Methodist Episcopal Church
The Methodist Factbook
1954   The Methodist Church
1957   "   "   "
1960–62   "   "   "
Handbook of Quadrennial Reports
1940–1960   The Methodist Church
Annual Report, Woman's Foreign Missionary Society
1884–1939   The Methodist Episcopal Church
Annual Report, Woman's Home Missionary Society
1884–1932   The Methodist Episcopal Church
Annual Report, Board of Foreign Missions
1939   The Methodist Episcopal Church
Annual Report, Board of Home Missions and Church Extension
1939   The Methodist Episcopal Church
Annual Report, Board of Missions
1940–1960   The Methodist Church
Annual Report, Commission on World Service and Finance
1941–1960   The Methodist Church

The board or agency structure can best be considered as a parallel and interrelated organization that stands in some tension with the conference line of organization. Without damage to the complex process of historical development, one can simplify the nature of the development of boards by seeing them as an outgrowth of voluntary societies formed to perform special tasks, and largely dominated by laymen who were excluded from the conference structure until 1872. Actually, the societies or boards developed with many ties to conference and episcopal administration, and they were gradually incorporated by legislation under the *Discipline*; but the board structure has never lost its relative autonomy as a task-oriented structure paralleling the conference structure.

The boards originated in agencies such as the Methodist Book Concern (1789), the Missionary and Bible Society (1819), the Methodist Sunday School Union (1827), the Methodist Church Extension Society (1864), and the Methodist Freedman's Aid Society (1866). By 1876 the General Conference had brought the Missionary and Bible Society under the *Discipline*. By 1872 the Church Extension Society became the Board of Church Extension and in 1876 was defined more precisely in the *Discipline*.

The structure of the Boards was stabilized in relation to the conference structure by 1939 with the merger mentioned above. The Board of Managers was constituted of all effective United States bishops (with vote) and members elected quadrennially by the jurisdictional conferences (ratio of one minister and three laymen for every n number of members in the jurisdiction), and its duty was to fix the staff and salaries, review staff work, and provide plans for auxiliary boards. The General Executive Committee was chosen by the Board of Managers and exercised its powers ad interim. The Executive Staff was elected by the Managers and made responsible for development and execution of program. The Auxiliary Boards, which are corresponding organizations in every annual, district and quarterly conference, were made subject to the parent board.

In his study of the *Office of Bishop in Methodism*, Robert Goodloe has given a concise statement of the significance of this parallel board structure that clarifies much of this organizational picture:

> Bishops are "itinerant general superintendents"; Board Secretaries are localized managers of specific interests. Each Board is incorporated under the laws of the state in which it maintains its headquarters and gives itself exclusively to the forwarding of the cause for which it was organized. These Secretaries are elected by the General Conference, are directed in their work by the Board which they represent, and are responsible to the General Conference, not to the Bishops.
>
> In fact, then, since 1860 there is a group of "general managers" in the Methodist Church, and also a body of "special managers"; and the general managers have no direct oversight of the special managers. And, what might be very correctly observed, as the work of the special managers increases, the general managers of the Church find their field correspondingly narrowed.[20]

A final stage in this organizational development illuminates the complexity into which these parallel structures had moved. By 1916 the General Conference undertook to coordinate the work of the boards with respect to budgeting and allocation of resources on an equitable basis through a commission on finance. Such commissions or quasiboards

[20] Goodloe, p. 178.

serving a coordinating function expanded rapidly and stabilized somewhat by 1956 (see Chart 2, Appendix). The joint committees and interboard commissions attempted to coordinate boards that the bishops could not direct and also to meet needs that did not fall under the responsibility of particular boards. Consequently Methodism exhibits an organizational development starting from what might be called a "preachers' church" through the lines of organizational structure—conference (preachers) and board (lay)—leading to parallel organizations. The General Conference admitted lay delegates by 1872, and the boards were never simply lay enterprises, but the parallel structure does reflect these two sources.

The comparison of the Disciples and Methodist organizations can be seen in simplified expressions of their organizational patterns in Charts 1 and 3 (Appendix). The significant difference is the parallel board structure in the Methodist pattern, although Methodist bishops chair policy-making committees and keep some control. The common element is the structure of task-oriented boards, commissions, committees, and agencies. Chart 1 would be too cumbersome if the commissions, committees and various boards were itemized; consequently, the real complexity of this organization is somewhat concealed. Some of this complication emerges in the consideration of the centralization of finance.

CENTRALIZATION OF BUDGET

Control of budget is a sensitive index of centralization. Several changes of distribution in budget figures from 1916 to 1962 for the Disciples of Christ as seen from the perspective of the local church, and comparable figures for expenditures of national agencies, indicate administrative centralization. (See Table 3, Appendix.) From 1916 to 1962 there was a 5 percent drop in the proportion of money raised by local churches and expended by the local churches. The proportion of the money sent to the national level from local churches that was allocated to administration of National Brotherhood (all denominational agencies recognized by the Convention) almost doubled between 1924 and 1960—from .28716 to .52981. (See Table 4, Appendix.) This represents a coordination of funds and expenditures through the national offices. At the same time, moreover, the total budget on the national level was increasingly drawn from other sources (compare Table 2, column 6, with Table 3, column 1, Appendix). This meant that funds were being raised from private gifts, foundations, and so on, thereby freeing national agencies for a role in creation of program without dependence on local units. Another indication of the process of central coordination was the creation of National Unified Promotion in 1924 to unify fund raising and develop an equitable allocation of resources. The effectiveness of this process is evident in the decreasing proportion of funds expended at the national level on administration of National Unified Promotion; between 1924 and 1962 the cost of administration dropped from 20 percent to 10 percent of total expenditure. Thus we see in the budget allocations of the Disciples of Christ a full confirmation of the centralization of administration.

Local churches of the Methodist Episcopal Church (as the principal partner in the 1939 merger) and the Methodist Church after 1940 contributed increasing proportions to episcopacy and conference;

between 1884 and 1960 this proportion rose from 11 percent to 20 percent. This is an appreciable increase in dollars, since the local church fund in 1960 exceeded 550 million dollars. (Centralization of funds and control of budget are even more clear in Table 5, Appendix, where the costs of the major administrative structures can be inspected.) The increased cost of Mission Administration in the national office from 3 percent to almost 14 percent of the total mission budget signifies a growing complexity of the task, improvements in training, allowances, and so forth; but above all it represents an increasing staff and activity on the national level.

Several other figures are interesting. The increasing importance of commissions and committees of the General Conference as compared to the cost of the episcopacy is evident in the increasing ratio of the cost of the former to the cost of the latter: from .04572 in 1876 to .95313 in 1960. Furthermore, the establishment of unified promotion through a central Treasury in 1924 did not result in reduced costs, as in the Disciples of Christ, but actually showed an increase in costs (see Table 6, Appendix). This problem has to be considered in another context, but it reflects the addition of promotional coordination without eliminating other promotional units that simply compound costs. In general, we see broad trends to centralized programming and expenditure, which reinforce the picture already drawn of the elaboration of administrative units.

Two forther aspects of the Methodist structure are illuminated by the allocation of money. Since the merger in 1939 there has been a marked trend toward increase of contributions from local church budget to subgeneral conferences rather than to the

General Conference; these contributions are largely directed to Annual Conference level, where the board structure has considerable staff and responsibility. Although such contributions were about equally distributed between subgeneral conferences and General Conference in 1940, by 1960 local church budgets contributed more than 73 million dollars to subgeneral conferences and 37 million dollars to General Conference. (See Table 7, Appendix.) This phenomenon of regionalism may be somewhat more general and should be explored in the United Church of Christ and the Presbyterian experience, since both of these bodies have strong conference and synod structures. Denominations within the federalistic polities may balance our picture of extreme localism moving to extreme centralization.

Another significant shift in allocation of funds occurred in the distribution of money between General Conference and episcopacy; although General Conference received only one-third in proportion to the amount allocated to episcopacy in 1941, by 1960 the allocations were approximately equal. This is actually an index of the attempt to achieve coordination of boards through quasiboards and interboards in view of the failure of the episcopacy to coordinate the board structure.

THE PROTESTANT PATTERN OF ORGANIZATION

Three basic trends characterize the Protestant denominations in their organizational growth: (1) elaboration of administrative staff; (2) centralized control of fund-raising and budgeting; (3) functional specialization through agencies and boards. We have traced these trends intensively in the Disciples and Methodist development. This general pattern holds for the rest of the sample with some variations; in fact, the range of patterning is rather well exemplified by the three Lutheran organizations. A brief consideration of these variants will make it possible to consider some general characteristics of this pattern.

The three Lutheran denominations in our sample were examined primarily on a regional or synodical level; budgeting, agency development, and staff relationships were considered on this middle level between the national organization and the local units. The Lutheran Church in America, the result of the 1962 merger of four Lutheran bodies, conforms reasonably well to the pattern shown by the Methodist Church, but with an organization much less complicated, partly as a consequence of organizational streamlining at the time of the merger.[21] However, the board structure tends to parallel the line organization of committees, posing the problems of collaboration and unified action. The centralization of board and agency work has developed to the point where many national representatives bypass the synodical or middle level and deal directly with local congregations. This power in the central agency is largely a consequence of centralized control of funds for mission development.

The Missouri Synod is a Lutheran denomination that originated with the Stephenites from Germany

---

[21] Statistics for the Illinois Synod, Lutheran Church in America, were drawn from the *Minutes of the Annual Convention of the Illinois Synod of the United Lutheran Church in America*—years 1920, 1930, 1940, 1950, 1955, 1958, 1960; the 1962 figures of the merged church, Illinois Synod, Lutheran Church in America, were from the 1963 *Yearbook of the Lutheran Church in America* (Philadelphia Board of Publication of the Lutheran Church in America, 1962), pp. 210, 250, 277.

between 1837 and 1847.[22] It is still an intensely German, ethnic communion, although a rapidly rising middle-class and intellectual elite, moving directly from farm to suburb, are offering a serious challenge to this traditional orientation. The Missouri Synod is a doctrinal or confessional body held in line by its directors and president in each synodical area. This doctrinal framework and ethnic base give the Missouri Synod a much more coherent religious patterning than other Protestant denominations. The agencies or functional structures are voluntary associations; unlike those in other denominations, these agencies have remained independent of the pastoral organization. Thus the pastoral direction and agency organization develop in association, and consequently agency development does not subvert the authority of the pastoral and teaching office. (This pattern has parallels in the Roman Catholic structure.) Moreover, considerable autonomy on district or regional levels prevents encroachment on local authority by agencies on a national level. The Missouri Synod deviates markedly from the modal pattern of Protestant organization; it is more doctrinally controlled, and it maintains communications through an ethnic communal network rather than through a national bureau of promotion.[23]

[22] Statistics for the Northern Illinois District, Missouri Synod were drawn from Report to the Church—Proceedings of the Northern Illinois District, The Lutheran Church—Missouri Synod, years 1920, 1930, 1955, 1960. The 1962 figure is estimated on the basis of The Statistical Yearbook (St. Louis, Mo., Concordia Publishing House, 1961), p. 174.

[23] This ethnic patterning gives the ordained ministry of the Missouri Synod a familistic character, as indicated in research by Ross P. Scherer, "Career Patterns in the Ministry: The Lutheran Church—Missouri Synod," paper read at American Sociological Association, Annual Meeting, Aug. 30, 1962.

The American Lutheran Church resulted from a merger in 1960 of Norwegian and German branches of Lutheranism.[24] The ALC combined the strong central authority of the Norwegian branch with the more balanced structure of the German branch, impoverishing local authority. The constitution and development of the ALC has subsequently intensified centralization and control almost to the dissolution of all intermediate levels of responsibility. A highly rationalized structure of committees (boards and agencies as we have been analyzing them) operates through regional directors paralleling the pastoral and representative structure of the region and controlling local activities. The net effect is to take over control of budget and program on the national level and to implement national programs on the regional and congregational level. This ALC pattern, one of the most highly centralized organizations in Protestantism, probably represents a temporary aberration in the unstable period of organizational revolution. By contrast, the Missouri Synod retains a pastoral structure and voluntary associations in nineteenth-century style.

The degrees of centralization, although not the forms of agency control that have been described, can best be seen through a comparison of local and national benevolences in the three Lutheran bodies. The Missouri Synod has maintained about the same ratio between local and national benevolences since 1920; the LCA has approached a 1:2 ratio in a

[24] Statistics for the Illinois District, American Lutheran Church, were drawn from *The Convention Report of the Illinois District, The American Lutheran Church*, 1961, pp. 56–58; the 1962 figures were from the 1963 *Yearbook of the American Lutheran Church* (Minneapolis, Augsberg Publishing House, 1962), p. 229.

moderate centralization; the new ALC structure is almost completely centralized. (See Table 8, Appendix.) Investigation indicates that the LCA is carrying considerable mission obligation toward inner-city churches in changing areas, whereas the more rural and ethnic Missouri Synod is spending its national funds for missions only in areas where the Synod has little strength.[25] The ALC has little work in home missions on a district level, and indeed, the regional director covering several districts in mid-America handled a budget of $1,400,000 in 1962–63. The difference between these denominations should not be exaggerated, but there is evidence that centralization of activities is in part related to loss of local and ethnic ties. In general, the development of national and agency structures is borne out in the Lutheran sample, but the doctrinal and communal base of the Missouri Synod retains much more autonomy on the middle levels of organization and protects the pastoral structure by confining the agency growth to voluntary associations. Data on the voluntary societies of the Missouri Synod would balance the picture somewhat, since these societies are the long-range source of organizational centralization in Protestantism.

With this broad confirmation of the emerging Protestant profile of organization, we can now turn briefly to several additional characteristics and problems in this new organizational style. Data from other samplings in this investigation bear out the broad trends but also highlight certain aspects of this organizational profile.

---

[25] Interpretations are drawn largely from interviews with district level executives of the three branches of Lutheranism.

ORGANIZATIONAL DEVELOPMENT

The organizational development of Protestantism has been largely a pragmatic, rational process. Paul Harrison's study of the American Baptist Convention documents this generalization for that denomination, and the present study bears out his findings.[26] Paul Harrison has noted the lack of ecclesiology in the development of the American Baptist Convention. This is another way of designating the pragmatic character of the development, for whatever the ecclesiological base, the various denominations have followed a roughly comparable pattern of large-scale organization. In the Lutheran mergers, efficiency of organization won out despite traditional differences. The deficiency in a theology of organization, characteristic of the Protestant tradition, has allowed flexibility and pragmatic norms to obtain in the development of organization. On the other hand, emerging problems of unity and coherence in organization create a need for a theology of organization. The controversy over the Faith and Order Working Paper, "The Ecclesiological Significance of Councils of Churches," and the intense debates at Montreal in the summer of 1963 over the ecclesiastical status of the World Council, are further symptoms of uncertainty on the theological status of religious organization.[27]

[26] Harrison, p. 209ff.

[27] For the discussion of these questions, see *Faith and Order Trends*, March 1963, Vol. 3, No. 2, "Churches, Councils and Unity?"; see also the working paper, "The Ecclesiological Significance of Councils of Churches" (The National Council of Churches, 1963); the meeting in Montreal, 1963, was the Fourth World Conference on Faith and Order of the World Council of Churches.

The process of adaptation according to the criterion of efficiency is exemplified further in Valorous Clear's study of the Church of God. The Church of God moved out of sectarian simplicity into a formalized denominational pattern; Clear's organizational study of this process is particularly dramatic. We see in the splintering and change encountered by the Church of God an intensified expression of the development many denominations experienced in the nineteenth century. Although the whole of this study has bearing on the Protestant profile, the following quotation summarizes the pragmatic character of this development:

Perhaps the most striking change has been in the area of formal control. Born in a setting of anti-organization, the movement in seventy-five years has developed to the point where the most recent *Yearbook* lists over two hundred names of persons holding office in the national organization of the group. Most of the first thirty-eight pages are devoted to describing activities of the various national and regional organizations.

This tightening of lines of control has tended to discourage deviant thought. The publishing of one's name in the *Yearbook* has assumed tremendous significance; it is a type of *nihil obstat*. If his name does not appear in the *Yearbook*, a minister experiences great difficulty in gaining an audience if he should desire to make contact in another state, and his colleagues in his home state hold him in question until he makes satisfactory explanation.

An additional factor in strengthening the lines of orthodoxy, a factor not yet fully appreciated by most of the Church of God ministers, is the recently instituted ministerial pension plan. A minister pays a portion of the premium; his congregation pays part. As long as he remains in fellowship his account is credited with both amounts; but should he be disfellowshipped he loses all the funds which were contributed to his retirement plan by a church. As time goes on, as men grow older, as the sums grow larger, this financial penalty on needy older ministers will probably be increasingly effective as a deterrent to deviant thought. And it is among the older ministers that the most stress falls in a religious group with a pattern of rapid change such as the Church of God has had.

However, changes in the area of organization have also served to give definition to the group. Homogeneity is more easily achieved or maintained when a committee is established to judge whether a candidate meets the qualifications established by the larger group. Although in the early years homogeneity was maintained through the close communication made possible by the smallness of the group, as the body increased in size and in geographic distribution the types of persons entering the group were *broadened*. This meant a diversification which has been partly brought under control by the formal organization, and particularly by the state and sectional registration committees which certify ministers' names for inclusion in the *Yearbook*.[28]

This pragmatic type of development is also evident in the large-scale organization of evangelism. Evangelism would seem to lose its authentic flavor when it becomes formalized through an organizational structure. In order to test the extent to which organization is a rather general phenomenon in the religious life of the United States, a study was made of the organizational forms employed by Billy Sunday and Billy Graham. Such organizational development is restricted by the central place of the evangelist himself; that is, the organization is built around a figure whose gifts and image are to be accentuated and whose limitations are to be minimized. Hence the organization of the evangelistic enterprise takes a different direction from the functional and task-

[28] Clear, p. 361f.

oriented organizations which we have been considering. Nevertheless, centralized control of finance, accounting, development of highly specialized staff, recruitment and organization of volunteers, and expert utilization of communications techniques are incorporated into the large-scale evangelistic campaigns of our day.

In general, the application of organizational techniques occurred under Billy Sunday and has been developed by Billy Graham. This transition to organization came at the turn of the century, as Bernard Weisberger has shown, and marks a transition to a new era in American religion.[29] To be sure, there are differences, for Billy Graham has access to mass media and can cultivate a national following, partly through the Crusades but largely through the intensive follow-up and promotional work of the Billy Graham Evangelistic Association. These are differences of degree, however; the similarity of style must be stressed. In both cases we meet a pragmatic application of organizational techniques to increase the number of "trailhitters" or "inquirers."

Despite the refinements in organization, the revival seems to become more costly; inflation, as well as the competition of other interests and opportunities, aggravates this situation. A comparison of the receipts and the number of "decisions" in the New York and Chicago campaigns of the two evangelists indicates that the average cost per decision in the Billy Sunday campaigns in these two cities was $3.47, while the average cost per decision in Billy Graham's comparable campaigns was $44.84. (See Table 9, Appendix.) The use of mass media which

[29] Bernard A. Weisberger, *They Gathered at the River* (Toronto, Little, Brown & Co., 1958), p. 270f.

contributes to this increased cost per decision is a necessity in a highly organized world, and it could be argued that Billy Graham's techniques are an inevitable adaptation to the increasing scale and complexity of modern society. Nevertheless, from the point of view of the campaign's central goal, producing converts, one must acknowledge the apparently greater efficiency of the Billy Sunday organization even allowing for inflation.

Efficiency is not to be equated with effectiveness, however. Competing with television, encountering a more secular mood, facing a rising social and economic level in the white Protestant constituencies, Billy Graham manages to carry on the work of his predecessor to a marked degree. Furthermore, the scope of the financial operation in Billy Graham's activities puts his enterprise in the field of large organization. To this extent, the most informal and personal religious activities have become a field of major organizational development in these decades of urbanized life and mass media.

MANAGERIAL PERSONNEL

Protestant organization has brought professional, managerial personnel into the religious picture. Large-scale, highly rationalized organizations cannot operate on a familistic basis. They require skilled managerial personnel who can decide on objective criteria about program and advancement. This creates a conflict between the "organization men" and the constituency; promotion becomes one way of overcoming this tension. Nevertheless, the emergence of managerial personnel needs further research, since it touches a wide range of conflicts in religious organization. Pastors experience this conflict in the tension between career and calling; the exercise of a calling requires some organizational structure, but large organizations tend to transform callings into careers.[30] Organizational staffs encounter this strain in local churches as the tension between cosmopolitan and local interests. Organization of religious activities on a centralized basis favors a cosmopolitan type who can move from one organization to another, whose skills are detachable and can be used with minor adjustment in any comparable organization.[31] Local congregations are interested in a man with local pastoral concern; the large organization turns the pastor's attention to the organizational demands—increased membership and fund-raising. The conflict between institutional structure and local values is accentuated with every step toward the development of large organization. Robert Rankin found evidence of intense feeling over this conflict of interests in a Methodist District in California.[32]

THE PROTESTANT PROFILE: CONGREGATION AND PROMOTION

The Protestant organization combines a pastoral structure with an agency structure. The pastoral

[30] Scherer notes that even the use of the term *calling* is weakened with the developing sense of organizational career.

[31] The study of personnel in the Church Federation of Greater Chicago indicated the high mobility and specialized skills which characterize this group; no member of the staff had been resident in Illinois when hired.

[32] Robert P. Rankin, "The Professionalization of the Calling: Functional Implications," paper read at American Sociological Association, Annual Meeting, Aug. 30, 1962; the materials for this paper were drawn from research incorporated in Robert Rankin's Ph.D. dissertation, "Religious Ideas and Church Administration: A Sociological Study of Methodism," University of California at Berkeley, 1958, unpublished.

structure is concerned with proclamation and teaching within the believing fellowship. The agencies have developed to maintain and extend the pastorate in a changing social situation; arising largely from lay, voluntary societies, they were gradually incorporated into the denominational structure. These agencies specialized in such tasks as church extension, education, fund-raising, and promotion. The pastorate is responsible for faith and discipline in the confessing communities, while the agencies are preoccupied with the organizational development and maintenance of these communities. The work of pastorate and agency should be complementary, but much of the time they are unrelated to one another, or, worse, at cross purposes.

The complementarity between pastoral direction and agency organization can break down in several ways:

1. The pastorate can hold its traditional authority so rigidly that agency development remains extraneous. This is the problem implicit in the Missouri Synod situation.

2. Pastoral direction and agencies can follow separate lines, thus running the risk of a dual organization and competing powers. This is the problem confronting the Methodist structure.

3. The agency structure, preoccupied with organizational extension and promotion, can take over the whole religious enterprise, directing all units toward denominational interests. This is the danger confronting many of the Protestant denominations.

The idea of a complementarity between pastorate and agency assumes that there is a *reflective* task of grounding action in faith (the work of pastorate) and a task of sustaining faith within the communities of faith and of communicating faith within the structures of a changing society (the work of agencies). In a static society the instrumental character of religious agencies can be maintained through pastoral supervision. In a rapidly changing society agencies of communication can easily supplant pastoral direction. The scale of agency development readily exceeds pastoral controls. This is a major problem confronting the Protestant denominations as in the third situation described above, where the religious enterprise is transmuted into promotion and organizational extension. Agency domination is a particular threat to Protestant denominations because many of them lack a principle of authority for religious organization beyond the "gathered" congregation. Hence, the dual task of religious organization—sustaining continuity in the community of faith and extending the impact of faith in the society—can easily dissolve for lack of direction. The proclaimed Word in the congregation may furnish sufficient organizational direction in a rural society. It is too local a principle for massive organizations.

In the nineteenth century agencies were very real vehicles of pastoral concern. The missionary orientation of that century saw the total enterprise as winning souls for Christ, and the agencies were implementing the essential task of the religious enterprise. This missionary understanding has disappeared, as Sidney Mead has noted, and the agencies are left with their own perpetuation as a major endeavor. The fulfillment of the complementary task of these structures may come, therefore, when mission and ministry are interpreted in terms appropriate to the twentieth century. This is the work with which the leading forces of Protestantism are now preoccupied.

Such a complete renewal of vision may preserve
Protestantism from domination by an agency bureaucracy or degradation to a struggle for power among
the agencies.[33]

Agency domination can be seen even more clearly
in the interdenominational organization. The lines of
communication in Protestantism are increasingly
horizontal—from agency to agency; the home-missions
specialists communicate across denominational lines,
as do foreign-missions specialists and other agency personnel in the fields of education, publicity, and social
action. Development of program and allocation of
funds for particular projects are informally effected by
communications between corresponding bureaus in the
federated structure. Hence, centralized policy making and budget formation may become formal rather
than substantial processes of planning and decision
making; effective processes occur within and between
agencies. The source of this agency power is often in
the large income that they control. Furthermore,
specialists within a particular federated bureau gain
support for their programs from their denominational
agency, which often designates its funds to the federation for specific agency purposes. This process
should not be exaggerated, since the denominations
carry a limited amount of the total federation budget
in most cases (22 percent in the Chicago Federation
in 1962), but appointments of personnel and alloca-

[33] The meeting of the World Council of Churches at New
Delhi called for an investigation of the Missionary Structure of
the Congregation as part of its report on Evangelism; this study
continued during 1962–64 with widespread interest in Europe,
North America, and Asia; the problem of missionary structure is
acknowledged to be one of the most critical questions confronting
Protestantism and bears directly on the problem of religious organization.

tion of the important funds above basic maintenance will tend to originate in the bureaus rather than in the executive offices of the denominations. Lay representation in decision making, except through agency boards, becomes very difficult under these circumstances.

Attempts at reorganization within denominations and especially within the National Council of the Churches of Christ demonstrate the dual character of Protestant organization. The National Council is a particularly sensitive mirror of this effect of agency organization since it was a formation of independent agencies that retained agency autonomy within the body of the Council. Planning and budget were largely controlled in the bureaus, a predicament aggravated by the role of denominational boards and agencies. The Council of Churches became, therefore, a cluster of competing bureaus. Bureau executives operated within two frameworks of authority and communication; they participated in the formal organization of the Council but retained effective power only through the informal lines of power radiating from the denominational agencies and boards. Coherent development of policy and program was, of course, almost impossible under such conditions; even personnel appointments operated from bureaus rather than from denominational authority.

The National Council of Churches reorganized its structure as of January 1, 1965, to achieve more centralized direction without losing the strengths that come from agency cooperation. The revised Constitution, adopted by the General Assembly at Philadelphia in December 1963, to become effective January 1, 1965, reflects the attempt of Booz, Allen, and Hamilton, Management Consultants, to guide the

NCC towards a radically reorganized, more centralized structure. Under the authority of a General Assembly, a General Board, and the office of the General Secretary, there are four Divisions: Christian Life and Mission, Christian Education, Overseas Ministries, and Christian Unity. In addition, there are three staff offices, Planning and Program, Communication, and Administration, which assist the General Secretary in his executive responsibilities. The office of the General Secretary serves as a secretariat for these bodies. Several thousand lay persons and clergy, working through more than eighty program units, comprise the assemblies, boards, and committees of the Council.

With the pattern set by this reorganization and centralized financial planning, executives of the member denominations hope to achieve more coherent planning within their own structures, through a similar process of centralization of authority and budget.

The Disciples of Christ, for example, are contemplating such a reorganization. The Commission on Brotherhood Restructure of the Christian Church (Disciples of Christ) has presented a "Provisional Design" for that body, considered at the St. Louis Assembly in October 1967, and scheduled to receive final adoption, after some revisions, at the Kansas City Assembly of 1968. The design provides for three main levels of operation of the body: Congregational, Regional, and International, with emphasis on those aspects which would enable movement toward constituting the Christian Church (Disciples) at the international level, with voting on the international level by both congregations and regions. The design involves establishment of a General Assembly, a General Council, and an Executive Council, and provides for the formation of such divisions and commissions as may be required, with individual boards to facilitate policy decisions of the Christian Church (Disciples), accounting for their work through regular reports of plans and actions to the General Council, which is to refer them to the General Assembly with recommendations for appropriate action.

It is quite apparent from the provisional design that the movement of this particular body is toward a greater uniformity of organization across regional and international lines, and an increased common understanding of roles, duties, and responsibilities of personnel.

The organizational problem of Protestantism should not be exaggerated. Administrative staffs and general operations are relatively efficient, at least as far as this regional sample could detect. The major difficulty arises from the irrelevance of much agency activity to the tasks confronting Protestantism in urban America. Clarification of goals will not be possible, however, until the denominations achieve clarification of their basic views of church structure.

Three

CATHOLIC DEVELOPMENT

In some ways, development of a Catholic profile is simpler than exploration of trends in the Protestant development; on the other hand, an intensive study of the informal organization of Catholicism might be far more difficult to execute. Our present concern with profile in organizational elaboration makes it possible, however, to examine the overall pattern of Catholic development.

The central fact in this organization is the diocese whose head, the bishop, exercises responsibility in all clerical affairs within the defined ecclesiastical jurisdiction.[34] The bishop exercises his authority

[34] Two general works provide basic information and interpretation of Catholicism in America: Louis J. Putz, C.S.C., editor, *The Catholic Church, U.S.A.* (Chicago, Fides, 1956) and John Tracy Ellis, *American Catholicism* (Chicago, University of Chicago Press, 1955); for a brief but valuable interpretation see

through two administrative lines. One line is made up of chancery functionaries—the vicar-general, chancellor and, in the largest dioceses, auxiliary bishops—who advise and exercise within a framework of legally defined duties. The other line comprises activities and organizations such as charities, schools, hospitals, cemeteries, administered largely by clerical functionaries and related to the bishops' office through priest-directors or chaplains. Organizational elaboration has occurred primarily in the associations and activities, although the chancery structure has also expanded. We can discriminate two lines of development, chancery and agency. The former is hierarchical and the latter is voluntary, or follows increasingly a voluntary association pattern as it is increasingly removed from the bishop. These are dual developments with varying types of interrelation. We cannot untangle the informal lines of influence within the dual organization since budget data are not available to give some indication of sources of power; only research on the informal structure of power would disclose the lines of policy that are actually operative. For the purposes of a profile, two kinds of data have been used: (a) a statistical study of the growth of the organization, employing indices of key officials in both administrative lines—chancery and agency; (b) the agency or associational development, considered separately as an indication of the pattern of growth. The data on association are drawn primarily from the develop-

---

Will Herberg, *Protestant, Catholic, Jew* (Garden City, L.I., Doubleday, 1955), Ch. 7, "Catholicism in America." The statistics on membership and functionaries are drawn from *The Official Catholic Directory* (New York, P. J. Kenedy & Sons, by years); reference is made to this as *Kenedy*.

ment of the former National Catholic Welfare Conference, now the United States Catholic Conference, the closest thing to a national organization of the Catholic Church in the United States.

THE GROWTH OF CATHOLIC ORGANIZATION

In order to provide a workable index by which to identify dioceses along the urban-rural continuum, and an index that, at the same time, could be derived from available data over the entire 1900–1960 study period, a simple "density ratio" was computed for every diocese in 1960 by dividing the number of parishes listed as having resident pastors into the square miles of territory of the sample diocese. Thus the Density Ratio represents the average number of square miles served by each parish within the diocese. (See Table 10, Appendix.)

As it happened, the urban dioceses that were selected from the 1960 evaluation were all in existence at the beginning of the study period—1900. This was not true of the rural dioceses. Nevertheless, about half the urban dioceses underwent division and resulting shrinkage in area, during the sixty-year period. Consequently, it was necessary to compare the 1960 density ratios with those in 1900, or at the point when the diocese first entered the sample (that is, the census year after its erection).

The highest density ratio in the urban sample is 181, for St. Louis in 1900; the lowest density ratio in the rural sample is 530, for Rapid City in 1940. This indicates that the division on the urban-rural continuum made on the basis of the 1960 figures is valid throughout the study period.

The notable changes in the period from 1900 to

1960 are in the increase in the median number of parishes per diocese (from 66 to 105) and the decrease in the median size of each in square miles— from 257 square miles per diocese to 108 square miles. (See Table 11, Appendix.) Although the number of dioceses increased by 70%, from 82 in 1900 to 139 in 1960, the bishop of the median diocese still was responsible for 60 percent more parishes by the end of this period. Hence the "span of control" increased, as smaller dioceses decreased —13 of under-50 parishes in 1960, as contrasted to 30 in 1900—and dioceses of over 200 parishes grew from 5 in 1900 to 19 in 1960. (See Tables 12 and 13, Appendix.)

The problems of complex organization are perhaps even more dramatically evident in the emergence by 1960 of such massive dioceses as the following:[35]

archdiocese/diocese	number of parishes
Chicago	437
New York	402
Boston	400
Pittsburgh	312
Detroit	309
Los Angeles	297
Philadelphia	290
Buffalo	267

The average number of square miles per parish gives some estimate of the urbanization of a diocese, although some dioceses include a hinterland joined to an urban center, which can make the figures deceptive. An increasing urbanization is reflected (see Table 14, Appendix). There is, of course, a consider-

[35] Kenedy, 1900 and 1960.

able range; for example, in 1960 the Diocese of Brooklyn averaged 0.8 square miles per parish and the Diocese of Reno averaged 3,250 square miles per parish. In 1900 the two dioceses of highest density were Newark (14.9 square miles per parish) and Boston (15.9 square miles per parish). The following figures for 1960 indicate this increasing urbanization in relation to these two dioceses:

diocese/archdiocese	square miles per parish
Brooklyn	0.8
Newark	2.2
Chicago	3.7
Boston	6.2
Providence	7.1
Philadelphia	7.5
Bridgeport	8.3

Our data on organizational growth need to be evaluated in relation to urbanization, since they could well be a simple function of overall growth. In order to test the relationship of organizational development to urbanization, a rural and urban sample of dioceses was isolated by means of a density ratio. In addition, certain offices were identified to serve as an index of growth. The number of parishes, estimated total Catholic population, and number of diocesan priests active in the diocese were used as controls to stabilize the diocesan samples. Figures on Catholic population in the Kenedy directory are not considered very accurate, but they provide an approximate measure of change at ten year intervals.

These figures give an overall impression of an increasingly complex pastoral and administrative development in the urban diocese in terms of increasing ratio of priests to parish and population per parish. (See Table 16, Appendix.)

This impression is borne out by the comparison of the number of chancery and agency functionaries in urban and rural dioceses. The notable fact is the proportionate increase of the agency functionaries in the urban dioceses over those in the rural dioceses—from 100 in 1910 to 1540 in 1960 for urban areas, contrasted with rural areas where 100 in 1910 had, by 1960, grown to only 450. At the same time, the number of chancery functionaries in the two areas—rural and urban—has remained virtually the same: 575 in urban areas in 1960, and 560 in rural areas in the same year. (See Tables 16, 17, 18, 19, 20, Appendix.)

The sudden change between 1930 and 1940 in the relationship of lay-organization functionaries to Catholic population in terms of numbers—in urban areas 835,000 per functionary to 284,000 in 1940, and in rural areas from 468,000 to 23,000 per functionary, is partly a result of the large increase in staff when a centralized office is established in relation to a relatively small population, number of parishes, and number of secular priests. Nevertheless, the increase in agency functionaries for the rural diocese is striking throughout the sample period. This period of rapid increase may well reflect a development of lay organizations moving out from the large urban centers.

The development of the Catholic organization is demonstrated with reasonable validity by these data, but more striking even than the relationship to urbanization is the intensive increase in agency functionaries, which we considered in the Protestant growth in terms of agencies and boards. These task-oriented groups are related to the chancery organization, as the indices of functionaries indicate, but the two are in a certain sense insulated from one another and form separate lines of growth. Coordination becomes an increasing problem with this pattern of organization, but there is no danger of the assimilation of chancery or pastoral direction to the agency development. Some further clues to this dualistic structure are provided by a more careful examination of the development of the agency line.

The Agency Development

In considering the emergence of the agency organization, it is essential to recognize the role of the chancery in the Catholic pattern of organization. The most crucial struggle in the victory of the chancery was undoubtedly the "trustee" conflict in the 1830's.[36] The issue arose over the role of the trustees who assumed ownership of property under the common-law arrangements of various states. Two types of problems emerged with the attempt to fit Catholic control of property into the common-law tradition: (1) questions of inheritance had to be settled when property was held by bishops or priests; (2) questions of discipline and control developed when priests or laymen assumed authority on the basis of their control of property. In brief, the congregational or parochial autonomy of the Protestant tradition or perhaps even the general practice of local autonomy and a voluntary conception of organization were infiltrating Catholic organization. The

[36] Henry J. Brown, "A History of the Church in the United States" in Putz, pp. 27 and 30; Harry J. Byrne, "The Financial Structure of the Church in the United States" in Putz, p. 103f.

question of title to property focused this struggle, although a similar localism emerged in the Kehensly struggle for ethnic Catholicism versus the universal character of the Catholic religious organization. The parish corporation method, especially as patterned on the New York law that allowed the archibishop to veto any act of the corporation, resolved the "trustee" controversy, and this pattern was instituted with minor variations throughout the church in the United States.

We have already suggested that the issue of chancery control can be generalized to the struggle against local identity, e.g., ethnicity, by the more universal structure of the diocese. This issue was not one of lay, voluntary control versus chancery and hierarchical authority, but it reflected the American stress on voluntary association, which played into the ethnic issue. The ethnic issue was resolved by compromise: nationality parishes were to develop alongside the territorial structures.

A related, though somewhat different, aspect of the struggle for control by chancery arose in the question of Americanization and the problem of an American Catholicism. As long as the bishop in his diocese formed the fundamental unit of authority and organization, all bishops were in principle directly related to the Holy See, and no American Church as such could emerge.[37] The history of Catholicism in America is in many ways a story of compromise between the hierarchical principle of direct line organization between the Holy See and the diocesan chancery on the one hand, and on the other the formation of a confer-

---

[37] Edward A. Ryan, S.J., "The Holy See and the Church in the United States" in Putz.

ence of American bishops with a somewhat voluntary character. We cannot enter into this long and fascinating story of competing ethnic groups, strong episcopal leaders, struggles with American situations so alien to past experiences of the Catholic church in a time of poor communication, and so on. The hierarchical chancery line seems to have won the day in a formal sense, and canonically there is no question about this line of authority. The American bishops did, to be sure, meet in plenary conference to clarify issues, make recommendaations for appointments of bishops, and develop uniformities of practice in administration, but until 1908 the American Church was administered as a missionary area by Propaganda or Propagation of the Faith under the Sacred Congregation.

NATIONAL COORDINATION

The bishops met annually from 1889 until 1918, but their decisions, guiding rather than authoritative, had to be cleared at Rome, and practice and appointments developed in these assemblies rested upon approval in Rome. In 1893 the Apostolic delegate to Washington, D.C. was appointed by Pope Leo XIII, and this papal representative has continued to work with the American bishops.

The hierarchical line of authority should be neither overstated nor underestimated in this American development; papacy to chancery remains the formal line of authority and is clearly formulated in the code of Canon Law; nevertheless by 1919 the annual assembly of bishops had become the originating structure and continuing source of direction for the then National Catholic Welfare Council. This

NCWC performed until recently as an entirely voluntary association of bishops, without juridical authority but with increasing importance as a coordinating body to deal with functional problems, such as education, publicity, and rural life, which are actually handled through agencies within the Catholic organization. These agencies have been related to the chancery through episcopal and clerical direction, but the associations have taken a relatively advanced role in the total development of Catholic life. Typical of such developments is the emergence of the National Catholic Educational Association in 1904 as the project of all those concerned with the welfare of Catholic education.[38] The advisory role of this association was later closely coordinated with the Department of Education of the NCWC, the director of that department serving as executive secretary of the NCEA. There is no longer, it should be pointed out, any official nexus between the NCEA and the United States Catholic Conference, whose derivation from the NCWC will be discussed later.

One gains a picture of the complexity and scope of Catholic education, and the formidable problems of organization it has encountered, from a brief review of the educational statistics.[39] By 1954 the total enterprise included more than four million students and more than 130 thousand teachers. Between 1920 and 1954 the elementary school pupils increased in number by more than 40 percent, and the

[38] Kenedy, 1960, p. 820; *National Catholic Education Association Bulletin, passim.*

[39] Frederick G. Hochwalt, "The Catholic School System in the United States" in Putz, and note that Rt. Rev. Msgr. Frederick G. Hochwalt held the post of director of the Educational Department of NCWC and that of president-general of the National Catholic Education Association in 1960.

secondary school enrollment increased by about 500 percent. The schools are operated largely within the parochial or diocesan structure, although some are affiliated with orders or private associations. The NCEA and the Department of Education of USCC have no executive authority in relation to the school system. On the other hand, the problems of state aid and of federal aid to parochial schools, practice in pursuit of Catholic values in educational materials, and other general concerns that cut across local authorities have been explored through these national agencies.

The organizational development of NCWC is one of the most significant forms of centralization in American Catholicism. At its inception in 1919–22, objections raised by some of the American bishops, sensitive like bishops everywhere to a threat to their jurisdictional authority, struck a sympathetic chord in the Holy See, where uneasiness has always existed concerning the emergence of national churches, and particularly over "Americanism" and an "American Church."

The net effect was the near dissolution of the whole structure in 1921, but, through the good offices of leading American prelates, an approval of the Consistorial Congregation was finally won in 1922.[40] In giving approval, however, the Congregation was very explicit about the voluntary character of the association, instructing that all minutes be reviewed by the Holy See, that even the troublesome term "council" be eliminated, and finally that the "agents"

---

[40] John Tracy Ellis, "The Founding of the National Catholic Welfare Conference and Its Final Approval by the Holy See, May 1, 1919–July 4, 1922" in *Documents of American Catholic History* (Milwaukee, Bruce, 1955), p. 630.

of the organization hold office only from meeting to meeting in order to prevent the development of a permanent bureaucracy.[41] Thus Cardinal Gibbons' hope for a "representative" and "authoritative" council of American bishops was disappointed, although the NCWC has in fact largely fulfilled this purpose despite the formal limits imposed by the Consistorial Congregation.

Chart 4 (Appendix) provides a rough schematization of the organization of the NCWC from 1954 to 1959, indicating the bureaus and offices that emerged within and alongside the departments.[42] In many cases a bureau developed in the secretariat for handling a special problem and then grew to such proportions as to emerge as a separate department: for example, Immigration, which handled more than 50,000 cases by 1954. The episcopal chairmen of the board were rotating offices, thus providing a distribution of responsibility. The administrative chairmen under the bishops generally provided the basic continuity of policy and procedure.

The episcopal committees which emerged within the Administrative Board, twelve in 1950 and nineteen in 1960,[43] included such activities as the American Board of Catholic Missions and the Committee on Motion Pictures. This phenomenon, even more than the administrative organization of NCWC, in-

---

[41] Ibid., p. 634f; for a discussion of the diverse sources of opposition to the Conference, see Aaron I. Abell, *American Catholicism and Social Action* (Garden City, N.Y., Hanover House, 1960).

[42] C. Joseph Nuesse; see also John F. Cronin, S.S., *Catholic Social Action* (Milwaukee, Bruce, 1948); also Kenedy for appropriate years.

[43] Kenedy, 1950, p. 74 and 1960, p. 852f.

dicates the national interests and task that brought the episcopal forces together across chancery lines and turned attention to the American situation. An urbanized society of large-scale organizations develops problems and correlated channels of communication that can be approached only on transregional and transdiocesan lines. The development of the NCWC was a realistic recognition of these facts. The increasing scope of committee structure within the administrative board likewise reflected the struggle to cope with an increasingly complex, national and even international web of interests.

Between 1947 and 1959, the Administrative Board was drawn largely from the densest urban areas. The excessive representation of the large urban areas, even though the distribution of bishops extended over all dioceses and actually overrepresented the rural prelates relative to actual memberships, suggests the dominant role of urban areas in the problems that have given rise to the agency organization. The secret ballot used in the election of the Administrative Board prevented it from becoming a self-perpetuating, permanent bureaucracy, and one can only assume that activity, attention, concern, involvement, and some influence entered into this close correlation of intense urbanization and the development of agency organization.

The NCWC has been reorganized, and decisions coming out of the Ecumenical Conference Vatican II have radically altered the structure and the scope of the two bodies which have emerged from this reorganization.

In 1966, the National Conference of Catholic Bishops (NCCB) became the episcopal conference for American bishops, with quasi-juridical power, in line with Vatican II's decision to invest conferences on regional levels with this sort of authority, offering a potential intermediary to the traditional hierarchical arrangement which dealt with jurisdiction in a direct line from the Roman Pontiff's international and universal authority to the local level of individual bishops and archbishops, with whom the Pontiff has concurrent jurisdiction, as indicated in Chapter III of *Christus Dominus*.

At the same time that the NCCB was invested with new authority, the secretariat was severed from it and given a separate status as the United States Catholic Conference, to be considered as a body with a primarily civil juridical vesture. Although the two entities are closely linked, and the membership is in fact identical, the NCCB is to be considered as a canonical entity, and the USCC as a civil. The executive board of the NCCB is designated as the Administrative Committee, and that of the USCC as the Administrative Board.

Currently a management consultant firm is making an intensive study of the USCC in an attempt to determine what organizational forms are appropriate to its new status: whether division or departments should continue, or whether its work might more properly be implemented in terms of units of activity; what increased flexibility might be brought about; what is the essence of the role of the General Secretary; in sum, how the secretariat can be most responsible and responsive to the world in which it exists.

The contribution of the prior organization was an important innovating and liberalizing function in Catholic development.[44] It also provided a medium

[44] Francis L. Broderick, p. 236.

for transmission of papal ideas across diocesan lines, as in the case of the development of the confraternity of Christian Doctrine as a major instrument for the instruction of nonparochial Catholic children. This development came about many years after command by the Holy See (*Acerbo Nimis,* 1905), primarily through the work of Bishop Edwin Vincent O'Hara.[45] This is an interesting story of the rapid spread of an agency structure through diocesan organizations after many years of work and primarily through the National Catholic Rural Life Conference. The papal-chancery line could not promote this program by mere fiat. Thus the NCWC represented not only a national agency structure for the American Church but also a channel of development from the Holy See to the national activities of American Catholicism; in other terms, the vertical structure of line authority was sustained by the complementary work of staff in a horizontal structure.

THE CATHOLIC PROFILE: HIERARCHY-AGENCY ORGANIZATION

The dualistic character of Catholic organization in America can best be expressed in the couplet hierarchy-agency. We have seen that the National Catholic Welfare Conference, and the two structures which followed it, are not radically separate from the hierarchical diocesan line of authority; indeed,

---

[45] On the development of the Confraternity of Christian Doctrine, see "Archbishop Edwin V. O'Hara, D.D., L.L.D.; A Biographical Survey" in *The Confraternity Comes of Age* (Paterson, Confraternity Publications, 1956); also Miriam Marks, "Teaching Christ in America" in Leo R. Ward, editor, *The American Apostolate* (Westminster, Md., Newman, 1952).

the governing board of agencies in one way or another stands in close relationship to the authority of the bishops. Nevertheless, we have also noted that the agency structure has a coordinating character that crosses the hierarchical line of authority.

The hierarchy-agency structure derives from separate principles of development held in tension through the episcopal office. The hierarchical principle represents the cultic, doctrinal and juridical line of development; thus the line of authority from Holy See to diocese, explicitly formulated in Canon Law, preserves the integrity of the Catholic faith as a sacramental system. This line of administrative authority has developed into a diocesan organization in the emerging urbanization of American life. The agency line develops in terms of functional problems in an increasingly complex national society; this functional principle produces an organizational development that cuts across the diocesan-territorial structures and yet depends on the authority of the bishops.

The problems within this dualistic structure deserve much more intensive investigation than has been possible in this research; such research would require access to confidence that might be possible only within the Catholic organization itself. Much could be learned from a study of this complex, and in some ways remarkable, combination of organizational structures; for example, studies of financial allocations and program development both within dioceses and on a national level might indicate the difficulties and advantages of this dualistic principle of organization.

Problems emerging from lack of centralized authority in the American Church may be offset by gains in stability in the ecclesiastical structure. Gains in efficiency within the national structure of Catholicism have to be balanced against dangers arising from too nationalistic an orientation for the American Church. The universal frame of reference provides a broader framework within which to evaluate gains and losses from the dual structure of Catholic organization. For this reason simple criteria of efficiency or adaptive flexibility, which might favor increasing the co-ordinating role of the USCC, must be counterbalanced with universal concerns for the unity of a world Church. These are the principles explicitly acknowledged in the Catholic organization.

In analyzing the organizational development of American Catholicism Will Herberg laid considerable stress on the role of Americanization through an Irish hierarchy. This emphasis is to some extent borne out in the present study since USCC is a distinctively American type of development within Catholicism. In some ways such an agency organization on a voluntary basis could have developed only in an American atmosphere, for it presumes an acceptance of pragmatic criteria for organizational development and a voluntary principle in meeting problems. Gustave Weigel has remarked on this pragmatic, activistic, and adaptive character of American Catholicism,[44] noting that the pragmatic emphasis on action has always been closely correlated with a marked piety and dependence on priestly leadership. His characterization of American Catholicism is borne out by the dual and yet interdependent patterns of organizational development. The recognition of the American character of Cath-

---

[44] Gustave Weigel, S.J., "An Introduction to American Catholicism" in Putz.

olic organization has to be kept closely in balance with the consistent centering of Catholic authority primarily in the papal-diocesan line of organization. This is an authoritative and yet voluntaristic structure —an American Catholicism.

The hierarchical principle has the clear advantage of centralized control in the development of long-range strategy. Kenneth Underwood remarked on the advantages of this principle in his study, *Protestant and Catholic*. Where the Catholic parishes were developing along with the gradual movements of population in Holyoke, Massachusetts, a rational plan under central control could be developed and executed. On the other hand, the hierarchical principle, whether in churches, industries, or governments, may develop a spurious sense of control, since lower levels of the hierarchy do not feed accurate information back and do not in fact implement the directives which are flowing to them. The net effect is an illusion of control at the top and informal control on lower levels. To some extent, the rectors in urban parishes have operated in this way during the racial crisis in recent decades. Perhaps in this way the voluntary principle has operated as a countervailing principle in the informal processes of the Catholic organization. However, our data could not extend to this area of informal flow of control and information —an aspect of Catholic organization which is much in need of investigation. Joseph Fichter published some materials on this problem in his studies of a southern parish, but fuller documentation might do much to offset a monolithic picture of the hierarchical principle in its actual operation. The present study furnishes considerable evidence that the agencies have operated to some extent on a staff principle of functional relevance—contributing new strategies and information as needed by situations in a more pragmatic way. Hence, the agencies have also offset the simple principle of hierarchy through a series of accommodations.

Four

JEWISH DEVELOPMENT

Understanding the organization of the Jewish community as a community of faith presents almost insurmountable problems to both insider and outsider. Here we are pressed even more self-consciously to speak only of profiles. Nathan Glazer expresses this enigmatic character of the Jewish community: "A social group, with clearly marked boundaries, exists, but the source of the energies that hold this group separate and of the ties that bind it together has become completely mysterious."[45] We shall attempt to penetrate certain aspects of this mystery, without pretending to unveil it.

The mystery of Jewish identity lies in its destiny and place in the American and world communities.

[45] Nathan Glazer, "What Sociology Knows About American Jews," in *Judaism*, 3 (1950), 284.

The Jewish community has not been assimilated into
American culture, whatever that may be; studies by
numerous sociologists concur at this point.[46] Acculturation has occurred, if by this term one means
the discarding of ethnic styles and linguistic patterns
for an Americanized style of life and worship. But
assimilation implies more than acculturation; it would
mean a transformation of the substance of Jewish
life, a dissolution of the distinct calling, a loss or
transmutation of the ethos and historical memory, a
substitution of American memory for the recollection
of "the People." The conflict between acculturation
and the maintenance of identity is a sharp one, and a
key to the contemporary situation of the Jew in
America. Institutions within Jewish life may be established to fulfill both of these purposes, and there
is a polarization on this score within the American
Jewish Community. Jewish parents who want their

[46] One distinct advantage for this investigation has been the
selfconscious study of the Jewish community by Jewish social
critics and social scientists; this was particularly important since
the present investigation had to depend upon prior research of
Jewish organization. In addition to specific references in the text,
the following works have been particularly helpful in giving different perspectives on the development of the Jewish faith in the
United States: *American Jewish Year Book* (New York, The
American Jewish Committee, Annual), which contains excellent
demographic and sociological materials according to general re-
search and current problems; Jacob Bernard Agus, *Guideposts in
Modern Judaism* (New York, Bloch Publishing Co., 1954); *The
American Jew: A Composite Portrait*, ed. by Oscar I. Janowsky
(New York, Harper, 1942); *The Jews: Their History, Culture,
and Religion*, ed. by Louis Finkelstein, 4 vols. (Philadelphia, The
Jewish Publ. Soc. of Am., 1949), esp. v. 4 in the concerns of this
essay; Nathan Glazer, *American Judaism* (Chicago, Univ. of
Chicago Press, 1957); Oscar Handlin, *Adventure in Freedom:
Three Hundred Years of Jewish Life in America* (New York,
McGraw-Hill, 1954); Will Herberg, especially Chapter 8; Mar-
shal Sklare, *Conservative Judaism: An American Religious Move-
ment* (Glencoe, Ill., The Free Press, 1955).

children to be accepted into exclusive schools or social organizations may at the same time be torn by the fear that their children may marry out of the faith. Assimilation in the sense of abandoning this tension and opting for a primarily American identity has occurred on the borders of the community, although the extent and rate would be hard to estimate.[47] Certainly the Jewish population level has remained fairly stable since the end of the major immigrations, and in view of the relatively low birthrate in the Jewish population, and the comparatively few "conversions" to Judaism within the United States, one can infer a slow rate of what Catholic sociologists call "leakage." Acculturation without assimilation is the situation of Jewish communal identity in the United States.[48] Jewish communal identity is preserved and communicated through a complex structure of voluntary agencies and associations; at the same time it is sustained and expressed through a sacred structure of symbolic acts and communal involvements. There may well be a unifying principle underlying both of these expressions of Jewish communal identity in the United States, but that principle has no organizational expression at the moment and is actually rejected on the ideological level by many of the most influential structures of the Jewish community. Unlike American Catholicism, Jewish communal existence in America has no single voice or representative agency.

The problem of the unifying principle of Jewish

[47] Mention should be made in this connection of the searching study of this problem published by Louis Wirth, *The Ghetto* (Chicago, Univ. of Chicago Press).

[48] Nathan Glazer, "Social Characteristics of American Jews, 1654–1954," American Jewish Year Book, 56 (1955), 11.

identity is not merely a matter of inconvenience to sociologists or theologians. It troubles the leadership of fund-raising campaigns, the welfare agencies, and most religious associations. Who speaks for the Jewish community? Who carries the ethos of Jewish life? What structures are pivotal in the coherence of Jewish identity? How does the Jewish community give voice to its political concerns when its status in the American community is threatened or when issues of Church and State impinge upon its life? These and innumerable other questions arise for the Jewish community and lie just below the surface of every fund-raising campaign.

The problem is familiar in the Protestant community; perhaps we can gain some clue to the best method of arriving at a profile of Jewish organization by recollecting certain features of Protestant life. The complexity of Protestant organization and the ambiguity of an agency that purports to speak for Protestantism arise from the voluntarism and pluralism within Protestant religious life. This is also true of the Jewish community. To say Protestant or Jewish community is to project a fuller unity and coherence than is warranted by the actual situation of either of these. Jewish life, even more than its Protestant counterpart, is thoroughly imbued with an ethos of voluntary association and local initiative. These are characteristics we associate with middle-class style in the United States; the Jewish people are, in this respect, more middle-class and more American than any other American group.[49]

---

[49] Glazer, in American Jewish Yearbook 56 (1955), p. 35; however, even such generalizations about the middle-class character of the "average" American Jewish person must be hedged with qualification; note, for example, the liberal political views

Whatever the roots of this middle-class style within the Jewish community—and some obvious sources come to mind: orientation to law and norm, emphasis on literacy, intensive experience of communication, and stress on verbal skill—the pluralism and voluntarism inherent in this style of life set major obstacles to centralization on a national basis. When Abraham Duker laments the impressionistic understanding of Jewish organization and the lack of rigorous studies of this phenomenon, he could as well lament the lack of clear subject matter for such a study.[50] There are no neat hierarchies; indeed, there are no comprehensive organizations whatsoever, and the resistance to their formation runs very deep within the American Jewish community. American Jews came to espouse the cause of Israel in the 1940's, but few were willing to submit their own lives to such a nationally organized community. Hence, the enigma of a Jewish communal identity with a pluralistic structure of voluntary associations will circumscribe our efforts at a profile.

Another distinction must be made in the phenomenon of Jewish organization. There is no neat discrimination of religious organization from the totality of Jewish life in the United States or anywhere else for that matter. This is in the nature of the case, because the Jewish faith reflects a calling that embraces the entire historical life of this people. We

---

and voting behavior of the American Jewish Community—a troubling anomaly in Gerhard Lenski's attempts to categorize this community (pp. 319–21).

[50] Abraham G. Duker has made an important contribution to the analysis of Jewish organization; see his "Structure of the Jewish Community" in O. I. Janowsky, and *Jewish Community Relations: An Analysis of the MacIver Report* (New York, Jewish Reconstructionist Foundation, Inc., 1952).

shall see in our consideration of Jewish religious life that the insulation of religious symbols from the public life of the people presents one of the most disturbing problems to Jewish culture in America, but in principle the faith of the people has meaning only within its whole historical life.[51] Particular cultural and social forms preempted a chosen place within this historical process, either the forms of intertestamental Judaism or the Yiddish culture of Eastern Europe; as long as the faith found expression in historical, cultural forms, any particular form might pretend to ultimate significance. However, the historicity of Jewish faith also involves the relativity of the forms in which it finds expression—not an historical and social relativity but a relativity in terms of the sovereignty of the One whose will demands obedience in every historical time and place. Consequently, acculturation can occur in Jewish communal life only as long as this does not abrogate the substance of the Jewish faith. The one thing that cannot happen is the dissociation of faith from the historical life and obedience of the people.

The definition of Jewish faith in terms of the

[51] Louis Finkelstein expresses this understanding clearly as follows: "Judaism is a way of life that endeavors to transform virtually every human action into a means of communion with God." See his chapter, "The Jewish Religion: Its Beliefs and Practices," in Finkelstein, *The Jews*, 4, 1327. Even this seemingly clear perspective within Jewish faith would not be uncontested; in fact, it is somewhat undercut by the distinction between vertical loyalty to values and horizontal loyalties to nation and community which is proposed by Jacob B. Agus in "Assimilation, Integration, Segregation—The Road to the Future," in *Guideposts*, 3 (1954) 498–510; here again the issue would not be one of principle since loyalty to the substance of Jewish faith would be unquestioned and the only problem will be method of sustaining that loyalty under changing social and cultural conditions.

whole scope of Jewish life complicates the question of Jewish organization. One cannot offer a profile of formal religious organization that reveals the organization of Jewish life in either a historical or a religious sense. Jewish faith manifests itself in both the religious and cultural expressions of Jewish community life. We cannot hope to glimpse the structure of the total life of the Jewish community, but we can recognize the major agencies that express its ethos and sustain its common life. To this extent we remain within the framework defined by Jewish faith, the only framework by which its own communal organization can be properly understood. In fact, this very definition of faith as embracing the total life of a community raises the question of Jewish identity within middle-class American culture; the Jewish community is at the very least a subculture with a sense of historical identity and calling—no less American than any other of the myriad subcultures within the society, and yet religiously identified in a distinctive and pervasive way.

We shall confine ourselves primarily to the Jewish development in the period since World War I. Several factors warrant such an arbitrary starting point: immigration slowed to a trickle after World War I, and the Jewish population began to stabilize. Whereas Jewish people comprised only 0.6 percent of the total population of the United States in 1880, they reached 3.5 percent by 1917 and have remained at approximately that point to this day. The major waves of immigration came between 1880 and 1917, but by the 1920's a native-born, second-generation leadership had begun to take over the agency structure of the Jewish community. By the 1920's all the elements were present for the shaping of the Jewish community; the ethnic institutions were rapidly losing their prominence, the agency organizations were multiplying and expanding, charitable enterprises were assuming major proportions both locally and internationally, and the new ethos of religious life was slowly making itself felt. Deep within this process one could trace the role of the Sephardic aristocracy and the German Jewish oligarchy (a lively account of this process is set forth in Stephen Birmingham's *Our Crowd*[52]), but the astonishing upward mobility of the second-generation Jews from Eastern Europe soon placed them in a competitive position within the agency structure. Although we miss much by starting so late in the Jewish pattern of development, we can pick up most of the threads in these crucial years. The new Jewish community, replacing the rapidly disappearing Yiddish culture, came into being in the period between the great wars and in that immediately following the founding of the State of Israel in 1948.[53]

In discerning the pattern of development, we will consider the fund-raising structures, the public information agencies, and the formal religious structure. These three organizational patterns are crucial to an understanding of the character of Jewish communal life and culture, although their selection forbids consideration of such important facets as the role of art in defining Jewish communal identity, and the very significant contributions of social scientists and social historians.

[52] Stephen Birmingham, *Our Crowd* (New York: Harper & Row), 1967.

[53] For the full sweep of these events, see Handlin, especially for an understanding of the role of Yiddish culture in the process of Jewish immigration and Americanization.

The Pattern of Agency Development

The character of agency activity shifted markedly with the Americanization of the Jewish community. The fraternal orders and benefit societies began to disappear in the 1920's, and were replaced by community centers with social and recreational activities. In 1913 the fraternal orders achieved a peak membership of more than half a million members; after that, they dropped steadily in number and in membership (by 1940, 345,000 members in thirteen orders.)[54] Some, such as B'nai B'rith, shifted their direction, taking on new functions and continuing to expand their local memberships and influence.

The community centers were developed as a way of easing the process of Americanization for East European Jews, as opposed to the West European Jews who were participants in the early synagogue movement (the Union of Hebrew Congregations was founded in 1873). At any rate, these community centers carried on social and recreational programs for the young under the direction of professional workers. In 1921 there were forty-seven such centers with 100,000 members, and by 1941 there were 234, with 435,000 members. Operated by the National Jewish Welfare Board, these centers are indicative of a widespread development of professional services.

From its earliest period of immigration, the Jewish community organized and supported numerous welfare institutions, but these expanded rapidly after World War I, and professional social work skills and techniques became prominent in the agencies. This expansion of social work agencies (using the term

54 Duker, p. 146ff.

broadly) and the corresponding professionalization of personnel removed the social work development from the central development of Jewish communal identity.[55] The indirect role of welfare agencies in shaping Jewish communal organization gives some warrant for focusing on the fund-raising and public information agency structures rather than on welfare activities.[56]

The federating of Jewish welfare funds is perhaps the most comprehensive expression of the unity of Jewish life in America. Charity and philanthropy are among the most characteristic features of the Jewish ethos in religious and communal life. The ethnic diversification of Jewish communities during the great immigrations, and the increasing diversity of local and overseas need for help, all contributed to a proliferation of diverse fund-raising programs in the Jewish communities of America. This was further complicated by the Zionist movement and the multiplicity of associations that emerged around one or another ideological aspect of this movement. This pluralism has not been completely overcome, as we shall see subsequently with reference to the public information agencies. Nevertheless, beginning with a federation in Boston in 1895, the process of federating welfare funds spread rapidly to most of the Jewish communities of the United States. By 1915,

[55] This pertains only to the major thrust of this profession and not to their concern; Samuel C. Kohs in "The Jewish Community," Finkelstein, 4, 1306 draws attention to this problem; on the other hand the centrality of concern with Jewish communal life is quite evident in The Jewish Social Service Quarterly, 17:1 (1940); for a balanced presentation see Herman D. Stein, "Jewish Social Work in the United States: 1920–1955," in The Jews: Social Patterns of an American Group, edited by Marshall Sklare (Glencoe, The Free Press, 1958), pp. 173–204.

[56] For a discussion of these agencies and associations, see Kohs.

forty-six cities had federated their giving, leading to a development of community councils to coordinate and allocate these funds; by 1941, 266 urban centers had such federations. Two coordinating agencies emerged as a consequence of this process: The Council of Jewish Federations and Welfare Funds (1932) which has already been noted, and the Large City Budgeting Conferences. These national organizations were to become major factors in the pressure toward a national coordination of the activities of the various agencies and associations acting on behalf of the Jewish community.[57]

The need for centralized budgeting became acute with the growth of overseas relief. The period after World War I was marked by a sharp rise in antisemitic feelings and propaganda, culminating in the tragedy of Hitler Germany. With each passing year came an increased need for overseas relief, further complicated by the Palestine question. Several factors contributed to the development of a united front of American Jewish people with respect to needs overseas. The Joint Distribution Committee (1914) intensified its activities during this period; by 1936 the major movements in support of Zionism joined in the United Palestine Appeal; by 1938 these groups joined forces in their national campaign as the United Jewish Appeal. By 1948, giving to all the charitable and philanthropic funds had reached a peak of more than 200 million dollars. After this point contributions dropped off, but to some extent needs abroad had also diminished.[58]

[57] Abraham G. Duker in Janowsky, p. 153f.
[58] Samuel C. Kohs in Finkelstein, pp. 1316–21; for summary figures on the annual level of charitable giving, see *American Jewish Year Book*, 63 (1962) 248, Table 1.

Before we turn to information agencies, attention should be drawn to the crucial role of the federated welfare funds and the United Jewish Appeal in symbolizing the identity of the American Jewish community. Participation in welfare giving is widespread in the Jewish community, extending far beyond any organizational or formal religious memberships. Jewish identity comes to focus each year in these campaigns; through a contribution one can express one's membership in Jewish life. Moreover, the overseas giving symbolizes the universal aspects of Jewish identity, reaching not only beyond ethnic and communal groupings, but also far beyond American identity. Such symbolization is very difficult to categorize, yet one can see the role of these campaigns in bringing coherence to American Jewish life. Samuel Kohs writes with strong misgivings about the centrality of fund raising in the Jewish communities of America, but his very concern reflects the importance of this process in the coherence of this community.

One can easily exaggerate the unity of this philanthropy, however; the information or community-relations agencies serve to complicate the picture of Jewish organization. The most powerful of these agencies, the Anti-Defamation League (1915) and the American Jewish Committee (1906) carried on their own campaign under the Joint Defense Appeal until 1963, when they launched independent campaigns. These agencies, along with the Jewish War Veterans, the Jewish Labor Committee (1934), the American Jewish Congress (1917, 1922, and 1938), and the Union of American Hebrew Congregations (Reform), engaged in various kinds of research, litigation, and educational work on behalf of the Jewish community. With the increasing antisemitic propaganda after World War I, the activities and budgets of these agencies grew rapidly.

The information agencies played an increasing part after World War I in clarifying the position of the Jewish community in the United States and the world. Between 1935 and 1944, allocations to national agencies went from 2.3 percent to 6.1 percent of total charitable expenditure; when one realizes that the total amount expended on charity almost tripled during these years, the increase is considerable.[59] The American Jewish community was dispersing rapidly into various regions of the United States, and American life was becoming much more complex. This was particularly true with respect to the task of transmitting an understanding of Jewish life to a second and third generation without the benefit of a close ethnic community. Publications, educational materials, propaganda, and extensive fund raising became more prominent features of Jewish organization with each new decade. Some sense of this proliferation of national agencies is given in the following figures: there were 26 such agencies in 1935, 50 by 1940, and by 1946–47, there were 268, of which 15 were founded before 1900 and 47 after 1940.[60] Moreover, some of the major information agencies had large local constituencies and rejected supervision by budgeting agencies.

One structure attempted centralization of finance; pressed by the Large City Budgeting Conference, the American Jewish Assembly was called in 1942 to bring various agencies together to work toward cen-

[59] Samuel C. Kohs in Finkelstein, Table 2, p. 1288.
[60] Samuel C. Kohs in Finkelstein, p. 1295.

tral planning. This group met as the American Jewish Conference, but attempts to make the conference a planning and coordinating agency caused the defection of B'nai B'rith, which realized the threat to its autonomy of such a scheme; finally the Conference dissolved in 1949, one of the series of abortive attempts to coordinate Jewish community-relations work.[61]

Under similar pressures and out of a desire for a more adequate strategy there developed a movement toward centralization within the community-relations agencies themselves. Many of these movements toward unification of agencies and activities came about during the war years, and such a coordinating body—the National Community Relations Advisory Council—emerged in the community relations field in 1944. Under pressure from the Large City Budgeting Conference, the NCRAC agreed to a fact-finding survey on the activities and expenditures of the agencies. A 1946 survey had led to much conflict and discussion, so the attempt was made in 1950 to obtain a neutral study under the technical direction of Robert MacIver.[62] The study report recommended specialization by agencies on limited activities in order to avoid duplication; coordination of

[61] Ibid., p. 1302ff.
[62] The original study was done by Martin Kohn and Arnold Gurin, A Study of National Civic Protective Agencies (New York, Council of Jewish Federations and Welfare Funds, 1945), mimeographed; the second major report by R. M. MacIver, Report on the Jewish Community Relations Agencies (New York, National Community Relations Advisory Council, 1951), offset; critique of the MacIver report by Abraham G. Duker, and an objective review of the total controversy by Selma Hirsch, "Jewish Community Relations" in American Jewish Year Book, 54 (1953).

budget and planning; centralized control of strategy under NCRAC, and increase in local responsibility through the Community Relations Councils in various communities. After several years of controversy, the Anti-Defamation League and the American Jewish Committee withdrew from the NCRAC in protest against implementing the recommendations, but in 1966 both returned to membership.

In terms of the organization of Jewish communal and religious identity in the United States, the failure to achieve centralized coordination of agency activities on a national level has very important implications. The pluralism of Jewish communal life has been reinforced by the failure to coordinate the agencies; these national agencies balance and supplement one another in their different perspectives on the crucial issues confronting the Jewish community. Professional domination of the structure of Jewish communal life would have required a centralized, coordinating bureaucracy. Whatever the rabbinate may have anticipated from such coordination, it never would have come about except through the power of the major agencies, which would, in turn, have assured the decisive voice of these agencies in the American Jewish community. The present situation may be less efficient, but it assures a certain balance of power between agencies and welfare funds, between rabbinate and agency professionals.

THE FORMAL RELIGIOUS STRUCTURES

When we turn from welfare and community-relations activity to the formal religious sphere, we are struck by the surface simplicity of the religious organization. This appearance is illusory, however, since the organization of Jewish religious activity is in many ways as enigmatic as the network of agencies and bureaus. Judaism in America exists in a kind of tripartite structure of roughly equal elements—Reform, Conservative, and Orthodox.[63] The Sephardic Jews of the earliest settlement align themselves to this day with the Orthodox tradition insofar as they preserve distinctive congregations. In general, Reform Judaism represents the most liberal transformation in observance and interpretation, while the Conservative movement stands as the mediating position in the adaptation of orthodox observance to an American setting.

A brief historical picture of the emergence of formal organization in American Judaism suggests the relative position of each organization in the structure of Jewish life. The Jewish community is very old on the American scene, going back to a seventeenth century Sephardic settlement; and in every phase of settlement, from Sephardic aristocrat to East European, the Jewish community found religious expression through synagogue prayer and communal life. The synagogue as a house of prayer was not a formal organization with professional leadership, but rather a communal organization under lay leadership, managed by a sexton. Rabbinic leadership was brought to America for its customary role of interpreting the Law in the life of the community; the rabbi participated in the synagogue prayers like

[63] The author is particularly indebted to Will Herberg and Marshall Sklare for this brief characterization of the Jewish religious organizations; see also Samuel G. Kohs in Finkelstein, v. 4.

any other man of the community. Jewish religious life centered in the community and its common struggle; the synagogue reflected the depths of that life but did not form its center.

Formalization of synagogue and rabbinic association is a sign that the communal bonds in Jewish life are weakening and formal structures arising as substitutes. Since there can be no valid substitute for communal life in Jewish faith, these formal structures remain ambiguous. Will Herberg describes this process as transition from ethnicity to religiousness in Jewish identity in America. Another writer sees it as transition from Jews in America to Jewish Americans.[64] This is the import of Will Herberg's stress on the struggle for Jewish self-identification in the larger American community. Religious forms, national agencies, and fund-raising campaigns contribute to the maintenance of Jewish identity. This total complex of differentiated structures unfolded from the Jewish community with its house of prayer, fraternal order, burial society, and Talmud Torah or communal school. As the communities of first settlement (to use Marshall Sklare's formulation) made their adaptations to American life and effected transitions to communities of second and third settlement, these communal activities were translated into associations and agencies. The fiber of the community weakened in the second generation; ethnicity dissolved as a bearer of identity; formal structures attempted to sustain Jewish identity in a complex, pluralistic situation. The key problem is whether an authentic Jewish identity can be sustained through formal associations and agencies.

[64] Agus, especially p. 503f.

The first major adaptation to American life came with the Reform movement under the inspired leadership of Rabbi Isaac Mayer Wise. He developed a prayer book according to American custom, promoted the formation of the Union of American Hebrew Congregations in 1873, established the Hebrew Union College for theological training in Cincinnati in 1875, and helped to bring together the rabbinical association of Reformed leaders in the Central Conference of American Rabbis.

This movement received doctrinal expression in the Pittsburgh Platform of 1885 adopted by some Reform rabbis—an extremely liberal statement within the tradition of German idealism. The movement toward a moderate position after World War I led to a modification of the Pittsburgh position in the Columbus Platform of 1932; this brought the Reform movement closer to the central position of American Judaism. Rabbinic and congregational associations were only consultative; authority remained with the congregation. This was no centralized bureaucracy with agencies, propaganda machinery, and coordinated budgets. This was the voluntary association *par excellence*; it opened communications within Reform Judaism through its seminary associations, scholarly writings, and publications. In an increasingly complex urban world, a network of communications was established.

The Conservative movement came into its own after World War I, although its groundwork had been laid with the reorganization of the Jewish Theological Seminary in New York. The Seminary, founded in 1886 to counteract the effects of the Reform college in Cincinnati, had little appeal as an orthodox training ground and reached the verge of bankruptcy at the turn of the century. Under the combined influence of lay concern and the genius of Solomon Schechter, the Jewish Theological seminary undertook the task of training rabbis for the new waves of immigrants—a rabbinate that could help in the transition from Yiddish culture to American Jewish life. This was the second-generation movement in vision and style, a movement that was to prove remarkably effective in areas of second and third settlement. The focus of studies and program developed around historical Judaism; English and Hebrew ranked together in this historical appropriation. The continuity of Judaism during American adaptations became the central task of the Conservative movement. With this inspiration the Rabbinical Assembly (1900) gained momentum, and somewhat later the federation of Conservative synagogues was achieved through the United Synagogue (1913).

Marshall Sklare's analysis of the Conservative movement has demonstrated its appeal to second- and third-generation Jewish people. When the Jewish community moved out of ethnic culture into some kind of accommodation to the American environment, the Reform program still seemed much too radical; the Conservative program was both familiar and adapted to the situation. Sensitivity to historical Judaism and concern for the second generation of immigrants led also to the Reconstructionist movement under the leadership of Mordecai M. Kaplan. This movement within the Conservative tradition attempted to link concern for historic Judaic civilization with a naturalistic philosophy. The added stimulus of Reconstructionism and the rapid upward mobility of the Jewish immigrants after World War I launched the Conservative movement into a ranking position in American Judaism; at the present time it rivals the other main traditions in Judaism and could outstrip them during the next decade. A strategy and voice of American Judaism may well come through this center position; certainly Reform and Orthodox Judaism modify their own traditions toward the center as the dual forces of accommodation and formalization put an increasing burden on religious symbols to sustain Jewish identity.

As one would anticipate by its deep roots in traditional communal Jewish life, Orthodoxy moved toward formalization much later in the period of Americanization. Between the world wars and after the restriction of immigration, several branches of Orthodoxy formed associations and achieved a certain coherence. The struggle of the Sephardic Jewish community to create an organization in New York resulted in a Union of Sephardic Congregations. During the 1920's the Yeshiva College (later University) undertook the training of an American rabbinate; its alumni, along with the growing body of graduates of the Hebrew Theological College in Chicage, developed an American Orthodox rabbinate. The Rabbinical Council of America and the Union of Orthodox Jewish Congregations represent a final stage in the process of formalization of American Judaism. The complex variety within Orthodoxy need not concern us here; nevertheless, this simplified schema of development should not be allowed to conceal the congregationalism and diversity within Orthodoxy.

The Jewish religious associations came together in the Synagogue Council of America in 1926, affiliating rabbis and congregations from the various branches of American Judaism, communicating on the problems confronting American Judaism, yet speaking for

Judaism only on points of unanimity. Rabbis and congregations have maintained association by protecting the automony of the local congregation and limiting the growth of a central organization. American Judaism has no counterpart to Protestant or Catholic organization, having proved intractably local in organization. This is in itself remarkable in an age of organization, and indicates the special role of a total, communal life in embodying Jewish faith.

EDUCATIONAL TRANSFORMATIONS

Educational development is a mark of the changed function of the synagogue. In the immigrant period, as indicated earlier, the Talmud Torah fulfilled a teaching function under the auspices of the community. By 1955 a survey of schools in the urban centers indicated that 90 percent of the children in religious schools were receiving instruction under congregational auspices.[65] All through the period following World War I educational facilities and programs were being expanded. National agencies for education, surveys, and elaboration of programs reflected

[65] Uriah Zevi Engelman, "Jewish School Enrollment," *American Jewish Year Book*, 56 (1955) 250. See Engelman's brief monograph *Hebrew Education in America: Problems and Solutions* (New York, J.T.S.P. University Press, 1947) for a discussion of the inadequacy of the congregational school which is criticized primarily as an inadequate, foreshortened version of the Talmud Torah with a serious attempt to establish Jewish education on modern terms (especially Chapter IV, "The Sodom Bed of Jewish Education"); congregational schools have continued to grow, as noted above, and concern for the quality of these schools has exercised both educational and rabbinical associations; see Sklare, *Conservative Judaism*, pp. 145–58, and especially the discussion of conflict between interest and building synagogue institutions and needs for general, Jewish education in the total community.

the struggle to cope with second- and third-generation phenomena in American Judaism. This activity came to focus in the elaboration of synagogue education. The basic increase in educational enrollment from 1900 to 1960 expresses this concern with formal training in the Jewish tradition; where Jewish population increased by a multiple of five during this period, school enrollment increased by a multiple of twelve; moreover, the weekday schools (meeting several times a week and teaching Hebrew as well as Bible and Jewish history) increased much more rapidly than the Sabbath Schools or one-day-a-week educational programs. The growth of weekday schools is also a good index of development of the Conservative movement, since Conservative synagogues developed weekday schools, while the Sabbath School of one day is more generally a Reform program. From 1948 to 1958 the weekday schools grew by 156.5 percent as compared to Sabbath Schools, which increased by 106.5 percent.[66]

Parental and leader expectations of synagogue schools bear out this interpretation of their function in Jewish life. Both parents and leaders see the function of the schools as primarily transmitting knowledge of Jewish life and culture.[67] Responses to a survey of attitudes undoubtedly reflect the value placed on knowledge in Jewish culture, but they also indicate the concern of parents that their children not lose touch with their Jewish identity and tradition. How effectively the schools are fulfilling these expectations cannot be properly assessed for several generations, because even immediate effects are not always helpful indices of reli-

---

[66] Uriah Z. Engelman, "Jewish Education," *American Jewish Year Book*, 61 (1960) 128 and 129, Table 1.

[67] Ibid., Table 12, p. 142.

gious education. Nonetheless, parents and synagogues have invested more and more of their time and effort in this enterprise.

One other aspect of synagogue life illuminates the function of religious activity in the total spectrum of Jewish organization. The communal-center movement developed in the area of second settlement to provide activities for the young as well as social and recreational activities for adults. Although the center program was originally directed toward the immense task of Americanization, as mentioned above, by 1945 this program had been redirected to the task of enrichment in Jewish life and culture. Such a transition seems very natural in view of the changed situation of the immigrant groups after one or more generations. However, the interesting development in this redirection was the fusion of the communal center and the synagogue into one common enterprise of education and cultural activity. Thus the synagogue becomes more and more central in the social and recreational life of the community, assuming many of the functions of the ethnic community. This concentration of activity and influence in the synagogue has stirred resentment among agency professionals, especially in smaller communities, but to some extent the fusion of religious and educational tasks in the synagogue seems inevitable in the attenuation of Jewish communal life.[68]

[68] The growth of the Jewish Center was notable between the World Wars—from 47 centers in 1921 to 234 by 1941; this corresponds to the second and third settlement process which we have been tracing—see Duker, p. 148. The fusion of center and synagogue, to the extent that it has occurred, is a more recent phenomenon and stirs resentment in smaller Jewish communities which depend upon the center for activities; see Max Arzt, "The Synagogue and the Center in Contemporary Jewish Life," *Judaism*, 3 (1954).

The period after World War II has also been marked by suburbanization of the Jewish population in major metroplitan areas such as New York; this process involves the dissolution of the multiplicty of agencies and centers that had provided services in the second settlement areas and opens the way for the concentration of social, educational, and religious activities under the common roof of the suburban synagogue. To this extent the development of the synagogue center corresponds with developments in Protestant and Catholic religious organizations.[69]

The role of the rabbi, as Marshall Sklare has made very clear, undergoes radical transformation with the new function of the synagogue. In the "organization" synagogue with its educational, social, and recreational functions, the rabbi becomes a professional leader of worship and a professional director of a complex organizational enterprise.[70] He becomes pastor and professional friend, fund raiser and administrator, director of a large staff of specialists, organizer of a school, symbol of the continuity of

[69] The social and recreational role of the synagogue is linked with the second and third generation phenomenon; Marshall Sklare has noted the lack of conflict with community centers because synagogues of the second settlement offered similar kinds of programs for their constituents, p. 138f; the fusion of recreation and synagogue seems to be intensified with suburbanizations, see *American Jewish Year Book*, 54 (1953) 98 and 61 (1960) 52, and Judith R. Kramer and Seymour Leventman, *Children of the Gilded Ghetto* (New Haven, Yale University Press, 1961) especially p. 46f; for difficulties in estimating suburban population in the New York area, see *American Jewish Year Book*, 62 (1961) 53ff.

[70] Sklare, *Conservative Judaism*, Chapter 6, "The Conservative Rabbi," which is an excellent analysis of general problems in the rabbinic role; the diversity of rabbinic types is well developed by Jerome E. Carlin and Saul H. Mendlovitz, "The American Rabbi: A Religious Specialist Responds to Loss of Authority," in Sklare (ed.), *The Jews*, pp. 377-414.

Jewish faith. This new role, still under the rubric of rabbinate, contrasts markedly and fits poorly with the traditional role of rabbi for which he is trained in theological school.

In Jewish tradition, the rabbi is interpreter of the Law, the code by which life is organized and directed to its preservation and fulfillment within the Covenant. He is not leader of worship, but participant with the men in prayer. He is not director of education and communal activity, although he is traditionally learned and called upon to teach. His expertise and influence derive from his knowledge of the Law and his capacity to interpret that Law in the complexities of daily life. Whether he is supported by a trade or the community or a patron or a wife, his learning and discernment enrich the community and keep its direction within the saving form of Torah.

The "organization" synagogue and the new role of the rabbi insulate him from the daily world of the Jewish laity and consequently from the task of interpretation of daily life for which he has been trained. The traditional understanding of the role calls for full attention to the Law in communal life; the rabbi actually has little access to the occupational and political world in which the Law needs interpretation; he lives in the private world of residential activities and feminine interests. Many rabbis do maintain contact with public life and exercise a very significant role in the larger community, but this task puts endless burdens on their time; the "successful" rabbi finds his attention drawn to the complex administrative and pastoral tasks of the synagogue. Finding himself in the synagogue rather than in the world, and driven by dissatisfaction at his isolation to an increasing degree from the public and occupational sphere in which Jewish men live and through which the destiny of Jewish people is shaped,[71] he is tending to become involved to a larger and larger extent in the community outside the faith-community.

The center of gravity of Jewish religious life is local, autonomous, voluntary, and to a large extent private in scope of concern. Religious symbolism maintains a memory of the Jewish people, keeping a sense of the past through which its identity is nurtured. The synagogue thus becomes the carrier of the tradition that had previously been borne in the common life of the Jewish community. If the full burden of Jewish identity rested on such formal religious association, the Jewish community of the United States would be weak indeed. We have seen, however, that Jewish identity is sustained by a configuration of agencies—philanthropic and religious associations—forming a network of communication and meaning which defies simple delineation.

The Jewish Profile: Community-Agency Association

A profile of American Jewish organization emerges from this consideration of the national agencies, the

[71] The general acknowledgment of loss of influence by the rabbis reflects their circumscription by the private interests of residential communities in which they are trying to make the synagogue central; see Jerome E. Carlin and Saul H. Mendlovitz in Sklare, and note that their optimistic conclusion that the rabbi may be a specialist in a community "built up around the Law" presumes an access to the public community of Jewish life which the rabbi has forsaken on behalf of the residential synagogue; in this connection, they might have pursued somewhat more carefully the special type which they call the Social Reform Rabbi.

federation of charitable work, and the new role of rabbi and synagogue. Jewish organization has its national networks of communication and strategy; it develops its own organizations for community-relations and fund-raising; it creates a variety of associations and bureaus for education and propaganda. American Jewish identity is sustained by these various forms; it is pluralistic in structure and more adequately described as a democratic association of various functions than as a bureaucratic organization. Three major structures organize American Jewish identity: propaganda agencies, promotional funds, and religious associations. However, this identity transcends these structures, informing the agencies with a concern for human rights, directing the funds to human need, and pointing the religious constituencies toward a universal hope.

The *national agencies* grew out of particular needs of the Jewish community within American society. These needs gave rise to diverse educational, publishing, welfare, religious, occupational, and community-relations activities. The agency was a product of particular interests and has become a source of interests, educational activity, promotion, and propaganda. This is said without pejorative implication, since this is the function of professional leadership; indeed, a similar interpretation could be given for the role of a political representative in relation to his constituency—he is elected to represent, yet he cannot lead in representing without guiding his constituency to a vision of what is in its best interests.

The agency organization thus assumed the ideological role for the American Jewish community—interpreting the changing historical situation in the light of Jewish struggle for identity and engaging in research on particular needs of the community. The ideological role is, of course, crucial to the continued existence of any community, since the understanding of the present situation orients the community to its historic past and guides it toward the future. The ideological task was assumed by the national agencies as heirs of the fraternal orders and local institutions. The resistance of these agencies to centralization therefore reflects more than resistance to change; the agencies arise from the diverse interests and perspectives of the Jewish community; they will centralize their activities only when the Jewish community approaches unanimity of interests they can represent. In this sense, religious centralization would be easier to accomplish than coordination of the ideological work of the national agencies.

The most important function of the agency organization is the maintenance of communications among Jewish leaders with respect to communal interests. This network functions both within the Jewish community and between Jewish leaders and the other major communities of American life. Such a network is, of course, crucial to the effectiveness of ideological self-definition, but it also provides the materials with which the ideological task is performed.

The agency structure of activity and communications, as we have seen in the Protestant and Catholic developments, is quite closely correlated with the functional diversification of activities and interests in the American community.

The structures of a complex society are too diverse to be handled by one agency. This need for functional pluralism expresses itself in the diversity of Jewish agencies. In the long run such diversity may be useful in strengthening communications within the

Jewish community. The biggest handicap in the present structure, however, is the rivalry and competition on the local level between the agency memberships. A study of fund raising in St. Louis indicated that such rivalry was very damaging to campaigns in the city, largely because it "jammed" communications and confused local givers. Whatever the final pattern of agency organization may be, its significance lies in its ideological self-definition of American Jewish life and the development of communications on a national level; its major contribution on the American scene, however, has been its continuous effort on behalf of human rights.

The other pair in the Community-Agency Association is the communal structure of Jewish faith in America. This structure has two functional aspects: charity provides a secular focus, and the synagogue furnishes a sacred focus. Charity and philanthropy provide a secular focus for the total Jewish community regardless of levels of religious commitment or observance. We can call this secular, although charitable works are if anything more central to religion in Jewish life than the more formalized activities of the modern synagogue. The United Jewish Appeal and the federated campaigns provide a unifying focus for the Jewish community that could not be achieved through formal religious structures or agency propaganda. Works of mercy in American Jewish life bring together local and national concerns, uniting the Jewish community in responsibility. The universal, world identity of Jewish faith is thus kept before the American community. The national scope of this fund-raising and the network of communications through which it is accomplished provide a second major organizational aspect of Jewish life in America.

The sacred focus of Jewish life is maintained through the new role of rabbi and synagogue; the house of prayer has become more and more a locus of Jewish communal life in transmitting the tradition to the young; the rabbi has become less a scholar interpreting the Law for the community and more the director of a religious institution. This problem of Jewish community—and it is a problem to sustain the integrity of such a community in America—has emerged out of the very openness of American society to Jewish participation in economic and public life. The loosening of Jewish communal life has placed an increasing burden on the synagogue, the Hebrew school, and the ritual forms of Jewish religious observance. As the rabbi finds himself standing more and more at the center of this religious institution, he is increasingly isolated from the public involvement of the Jewish community; his scope of activity is narrowed to the private concerns with nurture within the residential community; the expectations of his scholarly activity diminish with each passing decade; yet his symbolic role becomes increasingly important.

The task of the synagogue in the new Judaism has brought about a reversal of roles between the rabbis and the agency professionals. The rabbinate is limited largely to the institutional operation of the synagogue and assumes a managerial role. The agency professional becomes ever more deeply implicated in the public life of the Jewish community, interpreting its place in the American community and effecting a self-interpretation for the Jewish people.

Thus the ideological task falls to the agency professional, while the task of sustaining the Jewish communal network falls to the rabbi. These are both important tasks, but they reverse the traditional understanding of the interpretive and ideological work of the rabbi. This situation may well account for the tension between rabbis and agency professionals. Only the pluralism of associational life and the failure to achieve centralization sustain an equilibrium between these conflicting interests, enabling each to fulfill his task.

This profile of the organization of Jewish life is misunderstood if *religious* is interpreted to mean what happens in the synagogue or what is done by the rabbi and people assembled for worship. Religion within the Jewish tradition is all that bears on the life of the people, its faithfulness in commitment and action, its self-understanding, and its contribution to the world. In this sense, the Jewish faith is entirely secular and temporal in a way that Protestantism and Catholicism are not. At the same time the Jewish faith and religion are much more holy and religious than either Protestant or Catholic communities. Thus the profile of Jewish organization—a configuration of agency organizations, philanthropic endeavors, and synagogue activities—can be understood as providing a vehicle of Jewish *religious* identity. The center of gravity is now as always to be found in the Jewish *community* as a people with a holy past and a promised future. Whatever forces may emerge in the next decades of this "Adventure in Freedom," to use Oscar Handlin's telling phrase, Jewish organization is proving remarkably effective in sustaining Jewish *religious* identity through a very difficult process of acculturation.

Five

RELIGIOUS ORGANIZATION
IN A COMPLEX SOCIETY

Common features of the American situation have provided an external principle for the organizational development of the faiths. Rapid urbanization introduced complex problems of planning and communications. The diversification of educational, welfare, occupational, and residential spheres of activity called for a considerable diversification within the religious organizations. Although each faith-community shaped its own pattern of organization according to the dominant principles of its own ethos —congregational, cultic, or communal—the emerging organizational structures were very similar. This is the most striking feature in the organizational development of the major faith-communities in the United States. Similarity of situational demands and corresponding similarities of organizational development indicate a large degree of commonality among these faith-communities, at least on the structural level.

THE AMERICAN ETHOS: UNITY AND DIVERSITY

The common structural elements among the faiths should not obscure the differences in their organizational development. Those differences can be expressed most sharply in a few remarks on the significance of these faith-communities in the public arena of American life. In an essay, "Christianity and Modern Industrial Society," Talcott Parsons has argued cogently that the emergence of denominational pluralism in the United States represents a further differentiation of religious and secular spheres on the formal level and a deeper penetration of religious values on the informal level. American religious life is voluntary, pluralistic, and broadly accepted. Much like the family—and he means this in a very positive sense—the religious faiths operate through personal values and support an extension of spiritual values already grounded in the culture; they strengthen personal integrity and lend support to the rising moral expectations and individual responsibility that characterize American development. This interpretation suggests that secularization represents a deepening of religious faith and values rather than a degeneration of faith and morality in an orgy of materialism. Secularization represents the endorsement of personal and social responsibility in the public spheres of life, and the encouragement of voluntary, personal faith associations and activities in the private spheres. The broad principle is that specialization of activities can enrich social and cultural development when these occur in a context of broadened social integration of values and norms.

In this sense the three major faith-communities represent denominations of faith in the single, cultural context of American life. These are great denominational bodies with varying degrees of internal coordination. This study indicates that the similarities among them are striking, and Parsons' stress on the denominational form seems to be borne out. The Catholic denomination is the most unified, as we have seen, although there is far more structural diversity than is generally assumed. The Protestant faith has a diverse congeries of subdenominations within the total configuration. Robert Lee has argued in *The Social Sources of Church Unity* that the increasing number of mergers in Protestantism reflects an increasing homogeneity of Protestant faiths in correlation with the growing unity of social and cultural patterning of American life. Gerhard Lenski found homogeneity among the Protestant groups in his study *The Religious Factor*. The concept of a Protestant faith as a denominational body is not out of line. The diversities within the Protestant formulation may be serious and in the long run of some significance—for example, the special character of Negro Protestantism has already been noted, although this seems to be a transitional, cultural, and social phenomenon rather than a fundamental difference in faith. The Jewish faith is far more diversified in internal structure, but it also represents a broadly homogeneous structure in its organizational expression. We could argue for a fourth major force in American life—secularism—but its lack of organizational form and its shifting interests make the concept somewhat ambiguous. Hence the study of religious organization corresponds to a notion of a tri-faith denominationalism with organizational similarities.

Parsons' argument also makes value judgments about the deepening penetration of American life by the religious values of these faiths, and the broader institutionalization of the fundamental religious ethos within the secular spheres of American life. These are broad judgments about the quality of American life, and cannot be evaluated from this organizational study; indeed, there is deep difference of opinion on this issue within the faith-communities. Nevertheless, the stress on informal, denominational, and voluntary penetration of American life needs to be balanced with an appreciation of the scope and significance of the organizational enterprises these great denominations are producing. Two aspects of this organizational development need to be stressed in order to balance our assessment of the religious situation in the United States.

The maintenance of the sacred or pastoral aspect of faith requires increasing organizational strength in a complex society with pluralistic and voluntary structures. The organizational development of the major denominations—Protestant, Catholic, and Jewish —is integral to their task of maintaining proclamation, worship, and religious celebration in the diverse private contexts of a pluralistic culture. Hence it is not merely the organizational complexity of American life that has generated such large organizations of religious life, but also the task of promoting religious faith on a voluntary basis. Here the internal diversity of the three faiths is important, and internal diversities within Protestantism may become very significant. Organizations of communities of faith have to be evaluated in terms of their adequacy to defend and/or extend the faith without substituting their organizational activities for the central task.

The Catholic hierarchical structure seems most adequate to keep its organizational elaboration in line with the task of faith. Whether this is a viable alternative in the American context, even for Catholicism, seems uncertain, and there is some evidence that the structure is not so hierarchical as the formal organization would suggest. The Protestant subdenominations are having considerable difficulty in coordinating their agencies to the task of proclamation. The difficulty seems to lie in the lack of an ecclesiology adequate to interpret organization in relation to faith, and to legitimize structures of representation, decision-making, and goal-setting. For many subdenominations of Protestantism, organization is a contradiction in terms, since they anchor their position in primitive notions of the Church prior to its full organizational formation. For other subdenominations, as noted, this may be much less of a problem. Here the diversity in Protestantism becomes very important because some of its groups have a strong ecclesiological ground that can provide a pattern for Protestant development. The present talks among several of the major subdenominations become extremely important from this perspective, since they may provide a way toward a more coherent ecclesiology to bring organizational elaboration into line with the fundamental task of proclamation. In such a new organization, the formal elements sustaining strong organization may gain the upper hand.

The Jewish faith has the least organizational development on its sacral side, a fact that corresponds to the place of worship in the total context of the

Jewish understanding of faith and community. Nevertheless, the strains experienced by the rabbinate would indicate a general need for a much more unified development of national organization in which rabbi and agency professional could share. This may become possible only in the event of a decrease in the religious diversity within Judaism.

Even though one may entertain the hypothesis that these three religious communitites are great denominational expressions of a fundamental cultural and spiritual unity which issued in part from their heritage, each has a different relation to the American ethos. The problems and possibilities of these organizations can be understood more adequately as we recognize these differences.

The Protestant community has held a pre-eminent place within the American ethos until recent decades, as Will Herberg pointed out some years ago. The Protestant image had an unrivalled dominance until very recently. Although that situation may be changing, it may account for the fact that Protestant identity within the American identity was not nearly so problematic as Catholic and Jewish identity. The Protestant tradition in its dominant expressions could preoccupy itself with questions of promotions of congregational life within a larger, taken-for-granted Protestant community. Widick Schroeder has drawn attention to this phenomenon in several contexts. Our investigation of organizational elaboration would bear it out. The congregation and national strategy have been the two poles in Protestant organizational development, as promotion for survival and propaganda for influence have been its dominant thrusts. The lack of a principle of order has become a handicap only in recent decades, since Protestantism could assume an uncontested identity within a larger community. Pluralistic organizational developments presented no serious obstacles until the competitive situation of a tri-faith world emerged, as Will Herberg noted, and the complexity and secularization of contemporary society confronted Protestantism with intractable problems of survival and mission.

The Catholic organization has been a somewhat alien body in this voluntary society of pluralistic perspectives. This is not for a moment to say that Catholicism has not won an integral place in the American enterprise, but Catholic religious identity has been a serious problem. In the earlier period it was a conflict in the Catholic churches between Americanism and papal authority. In more recent years it has been a problem of agency developments coming to terms with the diversity and complexity of American life despite possibly limiting centralization. The centrality of the hierarchical principle and the care with which it has been hedged about in the many ups and downs of American Catholicism can be partly understood in terms of the precariousness of Catholic identity, in a voluntary, pluralistic, increasingly secular culture. It was not enough simply to be a good American. It was important to guard the Catholic faith as well, since Americanism could easily subvert or dissipate Catholic faith.

The relationship of the Jewish community to American identity was somewhat different again. It was not so much a matter of retaining Jewish faith in a secular world or a Protestant culture. It was rather a need to preserve the substance of Jewish community within a larger community. Jewish identity required a special community within the great society. The tension between acculturation and assimilation could never be relaxed, because temptations to assimilation were profound. This tension is illuminated in the volume *Jewish Identity on the Suburban Frontier* by Marshall Sklare and Joseph Greenblum,[72] whose subtitle tells the story well: "A Study of Group Survival in the Open Society." The position of the Jewish community in relation to the American community meant that the criterion of organization would center in the continuity of the community; hence, the significance of the synagogue would be adjudged ultimately by its enhancement of Jewish communal life. By contrast, one would assume that the pattern of Jewish organization would be radically different in Israel, where community could be taken for granted and problems would center more upon promotion and propaganda—the Protestant pattern.

It would be a distortion of the integrity of the religious bodies to reduce the understanding of their religious organizations to the position which they have held in relation to the American ethos. Nevertheless, this dimension sheds considerable light on the preoccupations of the organizations. The different principles of order which have guided these communities are kept in proper perspective when they are grasped in the larger context of the American experience.

ORDER AND ORGANIZATION

A tendency to agency control appeared in Protestantism; a cleavage between formal diocesan authority and operative agencies became evident in Catholicism; a tension between synagogue and agency

[72] Marshall Sklare and Joseph Greenblum, *Jewish Identity on the Suburban Frontier* (New York: Basic Books, Inc.), 1967.

developed within Judaism. We can comprehend these emerging problems more adequately when we grasp the different principles from which the three faith-communities proceed in their organizational development.

The Protestant understanding of faith is founded in the *hearing of the Word in the congregation.* Whatever the variations on this theme in the Protestant tradition, the gathering, hearing, and believing congregation forms the center of Protestant existence. The proclamation of the Word is *the* source of life. The pastoral structure of Protestantism receives its mandate from the Word in the congregation. Voluntary societies, agencies, boards, and committees have the task of maintaining, extending, and strengthening these congregational fellowships. Protestantism takes a pragmatic view of organization: as long as agencies contribute to the preaching of the Word, the administration of the sacraments, and the maintenance of pure teaching, they are justified. In brief, Protestantism upholds a dynamic principle of order—the disclosure of the Word with power in the community of faith.

The crucial significance of promotion in Protestantism arises from this dynamic principle of order. Organization becomes instrumental and flexible. For one thing, the congregation is a voluntary unit and can be maintained only by promoting support from the membership. Even more important, however, is the dependence of all organizational structure upon the authority vested in the congregational units. Protestant traditions vary in their interpretation of organizational authority, of course—Methodists originally vested authority in the preachers and Baptists in the baptized individuals, while Presbyterians are more federalist in structure. Nevertheless, the main-stream of Protestantism operates its organizations from delegated assemblies or conventions to which both pastoral and agency organizations are ultimately accountable—for funds if not for validation. Consequently, the organizations are forced to propagandize the congregations for support, and the technical staffs have to maintain control without adequate authority. These promotional efforts readily become the preoccupying activity of all Protestant agencies. Thus the principle of order—the Word heard and received in the congregation—easily leads to organizational superstructures preoccupied with promotion.[73]

It would be erroneous to reduce this Protestant principle of order either to the Protestant position within the American ethos or to a simple pragmatism in organizational accommodation. The Protestant principle of order is rooted in the dynamic understanding of God affirmed at the time of the Reformation. This reform was symbolized by stress on justification by faith through grace, the transcendence of God, pushed to such a point that Max Weber could develop a notion of "Ascetic Protestantism" without too much distortion of the phenomena; and the reassertion of the principle of Scripture over tradition or Church as source of authority. This con-

[73] Protestant denominations vary in their interpretation of authority for organization, and these variations create serious problems in church union. These problems are further complicated by historic conditions; for example, organizational problems in Methodism arise largely because it was meant to be an evangelical order within the framework of Anglicanism: see Albert C. Outler, "Do Methodists Have a Doctrine of the Church?" in *The Doctrine of the Church*, ed. by Dow Kirkpatrick (New York and Nashville: Abingdon Press, 1964), p. 12f.

figuration of Protestant thought, granting the variety and diversity within it, relativizes the place of churches, rituals, and dogma. This dynamic understanding of the Christian heritage persisted through long periods of formalism and Protestant scholasticism. The grounding of religious order in a dynamic relationship of revelatory power and obedient response, with all its variations in actual organizations, fostered a voluntary principle in religious community and an instrumental understanding of religious organization. This basic ethos, moreover, played a crucial role in the shaping of the American experience.

As mentioned earlier, the Catholic organization rests on a hierarchical principle of order. Catholic organization exists to maintain and extend the institution as a cultic body. Diocesan and agency functionaries justify their existence by preserving and extending the sway of these cultic forms. In contrast to Protestantism, the cultic activity of the local congregation derives its real authority and validation from the bishop's office; priestly authority is in this sense delegated from the pastoral authority of the bishop, and even the papal authority has its source in the papal role as first bishop in the See of Peter. This means that the authority of the organizational superstructure is quite clear; in fact, it is canonically so well established that a real question hovers over any other center of authority, such as a parish or an agency organization. The *hierarchy* thus preserves the institutional form within which authority is exercised and serves as final referent for any activity that purports to express that plenary power.

This Catholic principle of order likewise has its roots in a religious heritage. The Catholic principle rests on a dominance of rationality in the notion of Deity. Dogma, law, ritual, and religious forms gain authoritative status. The revelatory ground of the community of faith is truth disclosed within the Apostolic Church and its traditions. The authority of the Bishop of Rome and his fellow bishops is bound up with the continuity of revealed truth and tradition. Such a principle may allow for considerable latitude in particular organizational expressions and agencies to implement that plenary power, but there can be no question of a distribution of that authority in relatively autonomous congregations or individuals. The Protestant principle casts a shadow over all organizational forms in the name of a transcendent God whose ways are beyond man. Catholic organization preserves a church to which revealed truth was entrusted, holding sway over the faithful for their own sake and for the preservation of the true faith. In this respect, Catholic organization can have an almost unlimited flexibility in the instrumentalities which it may use, so long as direction and control are in the hands of those to whom it was entrusted by the apostles.

The Jewish principle of order is closer to the Protestant than to the Catholic. This is not surprising since radical divine transcendence or, in H. R. Niebuhr's term, radical monotheism, has been central to both Jewish and Protestant traditions. However, the Jewish community in its diverse expressions through thousands of years has laid far greater stress on the actualities of history than have most expressions of Christianity, which have seldom taken history very seriously. By contrast, Jewish religious life rests upon a people bound in Covenant to Jahweh, and held within his gracious promise as a special history. The community is the principle

of order because it is the locus of divine power. Whatever arguments and tensions may arise among rabbis,
agency professionals, social workers, fund raisers, and
teachers, the final arbiter is the Jewish community. This
community gives or withholds support. Communal continuity is the only validation of these various instrumentalities. Studies of the attitudes of the rabbinate
indicate that they evaluate their positions largely on
the basis of their influence in the Jewish community;
even the synagogue is a secondary point of reference
for the rabbi, since his success with synagogue activities must ultimately be evaluated within the Jewish
community.

The communal principle of order in the Jewish
faith leads to a wide range of activities and associations which comprise what we have called the Jewish
religious organization; we find that community relations agencies, social work, welfare activities, united
appeals, educational work, and synagogue activities
all contribute to the creation of a network of communication and propaganda through which the integrity of the Jewish community is maintained. In
contrast to Catholicism, the Jewish community has
refused to institute any central authority to coordinate
Jewish propaganda and centralize organizational strategy. While Protestantism struggles to keep its organization accountable to local congregations, the Jewish
community vests increasing responsibility in rabbi and
synagogue while giving them relatively little voice on
behalf of the total Jewish community. The community
is the bearer of faith for the Jewish people; here in the
history of this people God maintains his Covenant,
makes good his promises, and executes his judgment.
Agencies and instrumentalities that contribute to the
defense and enrichment of that community can win

support and honor, while those that fail to justify such support through their contributions to the Jewish community soon wither and disappear.[74]

RELEVANCE IN A SECULAR SOCIETY

Despite these fundamental differences in principles of order among the three religious communities, the common problems of development in a complex society, in which voluntary affiliation and pluralism of faiths were taken for granted, led to many similarities in organization. Another solvent among these religious groups has been the common concern to penetrate the structures of power in this secular world. This problem of relevance, and particularly relevance in a society of large-scale organizations not amenable to individual initiatives, has lured these religious communities to common enterprises and similar developments. The quest for relevance to the public realm is consequently a common denominator which may bring these organizations even more into a common pattern of development.

Ecumenical movement among these bodies has influenced two aspects of the contemporary situation: the urban crisis, shattering the common life of the cities, and the concern for world problems of peace, justice, and development which increasingly impinges upon the consciences of these universal reli-

[74] Seymour M. Lipset attributes the pluralistic structure of the Jewish community largely to the value of American culture; despite the interesting hypothesis in this article, the pluralism seems quite clearly a manifestation of the religious principle of Jewish identity—the community—in a complex, pluralistic culture; see S. M. Lipset, "The Study of Jewish Communities in a Comparative Context." *Institute of International Studies*, General Series, Reprint No. 130.

gious bodies, who have common cause with the world and must increasingly find both common cause with one another, and new instrumentalities for common action to promote human dignity. The secular society is more and more deeply entangled in a web of contradictions and complexities from which it sees no exit. Long insulated against these public concerns by a preoccupation with the maintenance of their own lives in the private sector, the Catholic, Jewish, and Protestant faith-communities are showing some signs of discontent with this insulation. If the concern is as deep as the impending crisis, we can anticipate some remarkable achievements in united organizational action by the three faiths. The common identity may well take precedence over separate identities in the emerging crisis. If this does, the voluntary principle and pragmatic approach will affect some of the more fundamental differences in order.

The second unifying aspect in this process of cultural engagement is the development of new forms of ministry to cope with the complex structures of an organizational society. Such new forms as industrial missions, campus ministries, task forces on human rights and peace can be carried out only by ecumenical ministries, since they are exercised in a secular context where differences of religious heritage are not relevant. There are already signs that these new instrumentalities can be effective agencies for the exercise of religious ministries on the broad level of problems touching human relationships and social justice. This is not to suggest that these communities are in process of blending their heritages or wiping out their differences in a single enterprise. On the contrary, the new situation in America in which the dominance of the Protestant ethos has been replaced by a complex, secular society may furnish the opportunity in which religious communities can enter with equal right and status upon a long-term engagement of common service: common because the three faiths have come of age in the society, achieving the parity which Will Herberg has discerned. If this be the case, common organizational developments may be anticipated, although the different principles of order will continue to direct. The Jewish and Catholic organizations are prepared for such a common venture because they have wrestled for a century or more to achieve a balance between religious identity and the American ethos. Protestantism is least well equipped for such a common venture, because its structure reflects an earlier era of Protestant dominance. Protestant religious identity is far more ambiguous. There is evidence that the common concern for relevance may accelerate organizational unity within the Protestant subdenominations. When Protestant identity does gain coherent form, ecumenical action by the three faiths may be possible in significant degree.

The American experience is a missionary venture of remarkable proportions. These religious communities have far more in common than one knowing their counterparts in the old world could anticipate. Their differences stand out as we penetrate their organizational structures. In the larger picture, their pragmatism, voluntary character, and common concern for authentic faith in a just society are striking similarities. In different ways each community has been pulled off center at times: Protestantism by survival, Catholicism by fear for its faith; Jewish community in self-defense. As such anxieties are overcome, opportunities for service and influence should open to these faiths. Such opportunities could be missed if organizational resources are diverted to unwarranted concern for separate identities. Particular identities are essential to religious faiths, and they call for a pluralistic society in which the faiths enjoy equality, if anxiety and self-defense are to give way to service and public relevance.

Appendices

Appendix A

Chart 1. Simplified Schema of Organization of the Methodist Church*

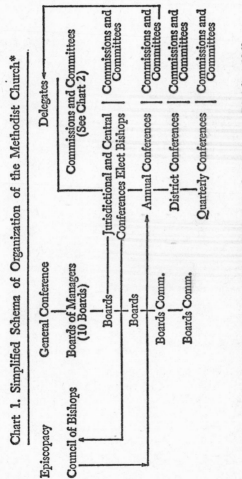

Episcopacy	General Conference		Delegates →
Council of Bishops	Boards of Managers (10 Boards)	Commissions and Committees (See Chart 2)	Commissions and Committees
	Boards ——	Jurisdictional and Central Conferences Elect Bishops	Commissions and Committees
	Boards	Annual Conferences	Commissions and Committees
	Boards Comm.	District Conferences	Commissions and Committees
	Boards Comm.	Quarterly Conferences	Commissions and Committees

* For recent definitions of Conference responsibility and Board structure, see *Discipline*, 1960.

Chart 2. General Conference Commissions of the Methodist Church*

1940

1. Joint Committee on Religious Education in Foreign Fields
2. Interboard Committee on Missionary Education
3. Commission on Records, Forms, and Statistical Blanks
4. Curriculum Committee
5. Interboard Committee on Cooperation and Counsel on Negro Education
6. Joint Committee on Cooperation and Counsel
7. Interboard Committee on Education and Lay Activities
8. Joint Committee on Architecture
9. Interboard Committee on Town and Country Work

1948

1. Joint Committee on Architecture
2. Interagency Commission on Audio-Visual Materials
3. Interboard Committee on Christian Vocations
4. Committee on Cooperation and Counsel
5. Joint Commission on Cooperation and Counsel
6. Interdivision Committee on Foreign Work
7. Interdivision Committee on Work in Home Fields
8. Joint Committee on Materials for Training for Church Membership
9. Interboard Committee on Missionary Education
10. Joint Committee on Missionary Personnel
11. Joint Committee on Religious Education in Foreign Fields
12. Interagency Committee on Social Issues
13. Joint Committee on Temperance Education
14. Interboard Committee on Town and Country Work
15. Church Survey Commission
16. Committee to Study the Relation of the Editorial Division of the Board of Education to the Board of Publications
17. Commission to Study the Advisability of Establishing a Methodist Headquarters

1956

1. Coordinating Council
2. Interboard Commission on the Local Church
3. Joint Committee on Christian Education in Foreign Fields
4. Interboard Committee on Missionary Education
5. Interboard Committee on Town and Country Work
6. Interboard Committee on Ministry to Neglected Areas
7. Interboard Committee on Christian Vocations
8. Committee on Family Life
9. Curriculum Committee
10. Interboard Commission on Christian Social Relations
11. Interagency Commission on Cultivation, Promotion, and Publication
12. Commission on Promotion and Cultivation
13. Television, Radio and Film Commission

* See *Discipline* for appropriate years.

Chart 3. Formal Organization of the Disciples of Christ (1956)*

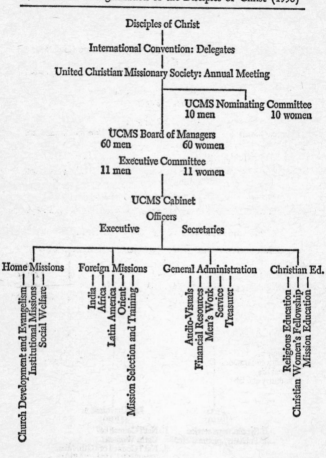

Disciples of Christ

International Convention: Delegates

United Christian Missionary Society: Annual Meeting

UCMS Nominating Committee
10 men   10 women

UCMS Board of Managers
60 men   60 women

Executive Committee
11 men   11 women

UCMS Cabinet

Officers

Executive   Secretaries

Home Missions | Foreign Missions | General Administration | Christian Ed.

Home Missions
- Church Development and Evangelism
- Institutional Missions
- Social Welfare

Foreign Missions
- India
- Africa
- Latin America
- Orient
- Mission Selection and Training

General Administration
- Audio-Visuals
- Financial Resources
- Men's Work
- Service
- Treasurer

Christian Ed.
- Religious Education
- Christian Women's Fellowship
- Mission Education

* See *Year Book* of International Convention, 1956.

Chart 4. Organization of the National Catholic Welfare Conference
(1954–55)

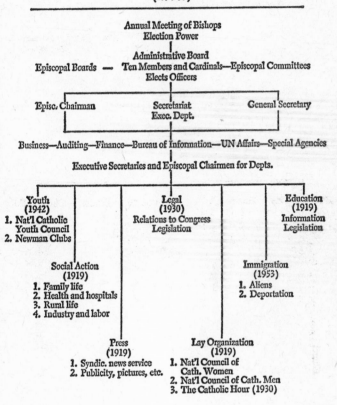

Annual Meeting of Bishops
Election Power

Administrative Board
Episcopal Boards — Ten Members and Cardinals—Episcopal Committees
Elects Officers

Episc. Chairman   Secretariat   General Secretary
Exec. Dept.

Business—Auditing—Finance—Bureau of Information—UN Affairs—Special Agencies

Executive Secretaries and Episcopal Chairmen for Depts.

Youth
(1942)
1. Nat'l Catholic
Youth Council
2. Newman Clubs

Legal
(1930)
Relations to Congress
Legislation

Education
(1919)
Information
Legislation

Social Action
(1919)
1. Family life
2. Health and hospitals
3. Rural life
4. Industry and labor

Immigration
(1953)
1. Aliens
2. Deportation

Press
(1919)
1. Syndic. news service
2. Publicity, pictures, etc.

Lay Organization
(1919)
1. Nat'l Council of
Cath. Women
2. Nat'l Council of Cath. Men
3. The Catholic Hour (1930)

Appendix B

Table 1. Disciples of Christ: National Staff, Churches, and Members, 1892–1962

Year	Number of national staff*	Number of "non-national" ministers†	Number of churches	Number of members
1892	10	3,897	7,850	700,630
1900	16	6,197	10,401	1,141,600
1908	21	6,662	11,307	1,285,123
1916	26	6,001	9,415	1,142,206
1924	46	6,383	8,877	1,359,884
1932	59	7,212	8,220	1,572,732
1940	68	7,448	8,070	1,669,222
1948	92	8,089	7,877	1,724,905
1956	131	7,498	8,062	1,930,760
1962	162	8,434	8,058	1,749,539

* These figures include technical staff members but exclude office secretaries; see *Yearbook* for appropriate years as indicated in footnote 17.

† Not holding office in a national agency.

Table 2. Disciples of Christ: Budget for Local Churches*

Year	(1) Total amount raised by local churches	(2) Amount of (1) devoted to local church expenses	(3) Amount of (1) sent beyond local church	(4) Amount of (3) to state and local causes	(5) Amount of (4) directly to state society	(6) Amount of (3) to national level	(7) Amount of (6) to national unified promotion	(8) Amount of (6) to nonunified promotion causes
1916	$ 6,590,960	$ 5,843,481	$ 747,479	$ 90,847	$ 90,847	$ 656,632		
1924	14,071,049	11,055,156	3,015,893	1,083,737	314,125	1,932,156	$1,884,996†	$ 47,160
1932	13,316,189	11,217,169	2,099,020	733,019	192,620	1,366,000	1,105,452†	260,548
1940	12,805,545	11,065,287	1,740,258	763,274	16,777	976,983	938,229	38,754
1948	34,720,511	28,092,774	6,627,737	2,707,060	42,561	3,920,677	2,079,161	1,841,516
1956	70,968,597	60,546,264	10,422,333	4,292,847	76,586	6,129,486	4,420,224	1,709,262
1962	89,097,370	74,673,718	14,423,652	4,785,545	7,658	9,638,107	7,820,693	1,817,414

* Compiled from *Yearbooks*; see footnote 17 for titles by year.
† United Christian Missionary Society (Unified Promotion created in 1934).

Table 3. Disciples of Christ: Budget for National
Agencies*

Year	(1) Total amount expended at national level	(2) Amount expended on administra- tion of national uni- fied promo- tion causes	(3) Amount expended on administra- tion of national non- unified pro- motion causes	(4) Total amount expended on national brotherhood administra- tion
1868	$ 7,569	no figures	no figures	no figures
1876	5,841	"	"	"
1884	52,637	"	"	"
1892	168,187	"	"	"
1900	425,581	"	"	"
1908	846,452	"	"	"
1916	1,288,770	"	"	"
1924	2,565,670	$ 504,362†	$ 50,471	$ 554,833
1932	2,816,925	505,212†	363,856	869,068
1940	2,825,628	543,730	57,464	601,193
1948	8,961,748	1,004,482	458,833	1,463,315
1956	18,205,553	1,777,081	1,191,053	2,968,134
1962	30,809,078	3,212,548	1,893,783	5,106,331

* Compiled from *Year Books*; see footnote 17 for titles by year.
† United Christian Missionary Society (United Promotion created in 1934).

Table 4. Comparison of National Agency and Local Church Budgets*

Year	(4 Nat'l) / (6 Local) Ratio of amount expended on National Brotherhood Administration† to amount of local church budget sent to national level	(6 Local) / (1 Nat'l) Ratio of amount of local church budget sent to national level to total amount expended at national level
1916		.50950
1924	.28716	.75308
1932	.63621	.48493
1940	.61536	.34576
1948	.37323	.43749
1956	.48424	.33668
1962	.52981	.31283

* Ratios drawn from comparison of Tables 2 (local) and 3 (national).

† Brotherhood Administration—all denominational agencies acknowledged by the Convention.

Table 5. The Methodist Church: Numerical Basis for Ratios on Administrative Costs*

Year	(1) Cost of the episcopacy	(2) Cost of the general conference	(3) Cost of missions	(4) Cost of mission administration	(5) Cost of missions with share of cost of central treasury	(6) Cost of mission administration with share of cost of central treasury
1868	(no figure)	(no figure)	$ 1,030,978	$ 35,000		
1876	$ 98,021	$ 4,482	957,645	62,657		
1884	54,047	29,086	1,179,363	69,321		
1892	92,361	39,832	1,863,313	105,805		
1900	88,597	79,127	1,911,752	124,286		
1908	94,614	15,991	3,720,147	256,913		
1916	206,009	152,631	4,067,976	248,011		
1924	(no figure)	(no figure)	14,791,713	818,875	$15,333,109	$1,360,271
1932	429,162	486,781	6,965,572	710,180	7,021,355	765,963
1939	398,075	(no figure)	3,238,727	353,106†	(no figure)	(no figure)
1941	482,680	136,522	4,233,918	433,295	4,257,449	456,826
1948	678,049	273,808	10,925,953	1,224,307	11,069,921	1,368,275
1956	1,099,944	1,031,828	25,490,587	3,133,156	25,843,282	3,485,851
1960	1,326,114	1,263,957	22,995,083	3,188,885	23,348,133	3,541,935

* Compiled from *Journals* and *Annual Reports*; see footnote 19 for titles by year.
† Excludes W.H. M.S.—no figure.

Table 6. The Methodist Church: Ratios on
Administrative Costs*

Year	(2)/(1)	(4)/(1)	(6)/(1)	(4)/(3)	(6)/(5)
1868	(no figure)	(no figure)		.03395	
1876	.04572	.63922		.06543	
1884	.53816	1.28261		.05878	
1892	.43126	1.14556		.05678	
1900	.89311	1.40282		.06501	
1908	.16901	2.71538		.06906	
1916	.74089	1.20388		.06097	
1924	(no figure)	(no figure)	(no figure)	.05536	.08871
1932	1.13426	1.65481	1.78479	.10196	.10909
1939	(no figure)	.88703	(no figure)	.10903	(no figure)
1941	.28284	.89769	.94644	.10234	.10730
1948	.40382	1.80563	2.01796	.11205	.12360
1956	.93807	2.84847	3.16912	.12291	.13488
1960	.95313	2.40468	2.67091	.13868	.15170

* See Table 5 for designations of numbers in parentheses.

Table 7. The Methodist Church: Contributions from
Local Churches to Subgeneral and General
Conferences*

Year	Amount to subgeneral conferences	Amount to general conference
1940	$ 8,303,163	$ 8,377,736
1948	24,046,680	14,674,888
1960	73,179,445	36,955,779

* Compiled from *Journal*; see footnote 19 for titles.

Table 8. Benevolence per Member for Regional and
National Purposes in the Lutheran Church of America,
Missouri Synod, and American Lutheran Church*

Year	L.C.A. Synod	L.C.A. National	M.S. District	M.S. National	A.L.C. District	A.L.C. National
1920	$ .80	$1.02	$ 1.10	$ .90		
1930	.97	1.73	2.00	1.81		
1940	.38	.76				
1950	1.67	2.68				
1955	2.89	3.40				
1958	5.30	4.71				
1961			10.00	10.50	$.32	$6.20
1963	4.64	7.14			.36	7.96

* L.C.A. and A.L.C. figures are compiled from regional annual
reports for appropriate years (see footnotes 21 and 24); M.S.
statistics are compiled from 1920 and 1961 *Statistical Yearbooks*.

Table 9. Receipts and Decisions in the New York and Chicago Evangelistic Campaigns of Billy Sunday and Billy Graham

	Billy Sunday			Billy Graham		
	Receipts	Decisions	Date	Receipts	Decisions	Date
New York	$320,669[a]	98,264[c]	(1917)	$2,500,000[e]	56,767[g]	(1957)
Chicago	191,000[b]	49,165[d]	(1918)	783,219[f]	16,451[h]	(1962)
Total	$511,669	147,429		$3,283,219	73,218	
Average cost to cities per decision		$3.47			$44.84	

a. William G. McLoughlin, Jr., *Billy Sunday Was His Real Name* (Chicago University Press, Chicago, 1955), pp. 109, 174.
b. *Ibid.*, pp. 109, 115.
c. *Ibid.*, p. 103.
d. *Ibid.*, p. 103.
e. William G. McLoughlin, *Billy Graham, Revivalist in a Secular Age* (New York, Ronald Press, 1960), p. 149.
f. Official Report on Billy Graham Greater Chicago Crusade.
g. McLoughlin, p. 149.
h. Official Report on Billy Graham Greater Chicago Crusade.

Table 10. Density Ratios* of Sample Dioceses at Beginning and End of Study

Urban sample**	1900	1960	Rural sample	1900	1960
Boston	15	0	Amarillo (1930)	3,300	1,001
Brooklyn	7	0.8	Atlanta (1960)	850	760
Chicago	46	3.7	Baker (1910)	4,700	2,300
Cleveland	75	15	Boise (1910)	3,500	1,550
Detroit	142	17	Charleston (1900)	3,300	500
Hartford	37	12	Cheyenne (1900)	8,100	2,640
Milwaukee	60	18	El Paso (1920)	1,950	1,030
Newark	14		Gallup (1940)	4,400	2,440
New York	17	12	Grand Island (1920)	920	740
Philadelphia	23	2.2	Great Falls (1910)	4,300	1,430
Pittsburgh	58	13	Helena (1900)	4,800	940
Providence	27	7	Nashville (1900)	1,900	564
St. Louis	181	25	Pueblo (1950)	1,200	865
St. Paul	100	29	Rapid City (1940)	530	642
Trenton	70	21	Reno (1940)	6,400	3,250
			Salt Lake City (1900)	17,000	2,500
			Savannah (1900)	4,800	1,040
			Tucson (1900)	8,200	620
			Yakima (1960)	660	650

* The density ratio represents the average number of square miles served by each parish within the diocese.

** Because two quintile criteria were used for identifying each sample, the resulting number of dioceses in each sample is not the same; that is, fewer dioceses in the urban sample qualified under both the density and number of parishes criteria than in the rural sample.

Table 11. Summary of Parish-Diocesan Growth Pattern,
1900–60*

	1900	1920	1940	1960
Number of dioceses	82	100	112	139
Total N of parishes	6,530	10,192	13,094	16,778
Median N of parishes per diocese	66	85	90	105
Average N of parishes per diocese	79.6	101.9	116.9	120.7
Median size of parishes (sq. mi.)	257	233	120	108
Average size of parishes (sq. mi.)	540	345	275	216

* Kenedy, 1901, 1920, 1940, 1960, *passim.*

Table 10 identifies all the dioceses used in each sample and displays the two density ratios. The parentheses after the dioceses in the rural sample indicate the census year in which the diocese first entered the sample and consequently the year for which the first of the two density ratios is computed.

Table 12. Pattern of Diocesan Growth by Number of
Parishes in Diocese, 1900–60*

Number of parishes in diocese	Number of dioceses			
	1900	1920	1940	1960
Under 50	30	25	19	13
50 to 100	27	36	44	52
100 to 150	15	19	21	44
150 to 200	5	8	9	11
200 and over	5	12	19	19

* Kenedy, 1901, 1921, 1940, 1960, *passim.*

Table 13. Percentage Distribution by Number of
Parishes in Diocese, 1900–60*

Number of parishes in diocese	Percentage of total dioceses			
	1900	1920	1940	1960
Under 50	36.6	25.0	17.0	9.4
50 to 100	32.9	36.0	39.3	37.4
100 to 150	18.3	19.0	18.7	31.6
150 to 200	6.1	8.0	8.0	7.9
200 and over	6.1	12.0	17.0	13.7

* Kenedy, 1901, 1920, 1940, 1960, *passim.*

Table 14. Pattern of Diocesan Growth by Average
Square Miles per Parish in Each Diocese*

Average square miles per parish	Number of dioceses			
	1900	1920	1940	1960
Under 20	3	4	8	19
20 to 100	18	10	28	44
100 to 200	15	37	23	18
200 to 300	7	14	15	16
300 to 500	5	11	14	14
500 to 1,000	4	17	17	15
1,000 and over	30	7	7	13

* Kenedy, 1901, 1920, 1940, 1960, *passim.*

Table 15. Priests, Parishes, and Population: Urban and
Rural Groups, 1900–60*

	1900	1910	1920	1930	1940	1950	1960
Urban							
Total priests per parish[a]	2.08	2.15	2.38	2.68	3.24	4.10	4.61
Diocesan priests per parish[b]	1.59	1.60	1.78	1.88	2.38	2.46	2.54
Catholic pop. per parish	2,680	2,400	2,570	2,480	3,390	2,960	3,820
Catholic pop. per priest[a]	1,280	1,130	1,080	925	854	720	830
Catholic pop. per diocesan priest[b]	1,680	1,490	1,440	1,320	1,160	1,200	1,510
Rural							
Total priests per parish[a]	1.78	2.06	1.68	1.83	1.83	2.10	2.30
Diocesan priests per parish[b]	1.24	1.36	1.10	1.17	1.25	1.19	1.26
Catholic pop. per parish	1,460	1,040	1,105	1,080	1,000	1,150	1,540
Catholic pop. per priest[a]	820	510	652	625	527	546	670
Catholic pop. per diocesan priest[b]	1,175	770	1,000	910	802	965	1,220

* Kenedy, 1901, 1910, 1920, 1930, 1940, 1950, 1960, *passim*.
  a. This figure includes all priests, secular (diocesan) and religious orders, and includes priests associated with colleges, uni-
versities, seminaries, high schools, and other non-parochial
functions.
  b. This figure includes only secular (diocesan) priests, although
it includes those secular priests associated with non-diocesan
functions. It does not include religious order priests.

Table 16. Number of Primary Bureaucratic
Functionaries per Diocese, Urban and Rural, 1900–60*

	1900	1910	1920	1930	1940	1950	1960
All functionaries[a]							
Urban	2.7	3.3	5.0	8.1	11.6	15.9	23.2
Rural	1.1	1.3	2.5	3.0	4.3	8.1	8.7
Chancel functionaries[b]							
Urban	2.7	3.1	4.5	7.3	9.2	11.6	15.5
Rural	1.1	1.3	1.7	2.3	2.7	4.4	5.1
Agency functionaries[c]							
Urban	0	0.2	0.5	0.8	2.4	4.3	7.7
Rural	0	0	0.8	0.7	1.6	3.8	3.6

* Kenedy, 1901, 1910, 1920, 1930, 1940, 1950, 1960, *passim*.

a. Sum of functionaries included in notes (b) and (c).

b. Sum of vicars-general, chancellors, vice-chancellors, assistant chancellors, auxiliary bishops, and the diocesan directors and assistant directors of Catholic charities, hospitals, schools, and cemeteries.

c. Sum of diocesan directors and assistant directors of Confraternity of Christian Doctrine, Catholic Youth Organizations, or similar organizations, CANA, Family Life groups, Councils of Catholic Men, Councils of Catholic Women, Catholic Action Federations, Rural Life Conference, Legion of Mary.

Table 17. Change in Primary Bureaucratic
Functionaries per Diocese, Urban and Rural, 1900–60

	1900	1910	1920	1930	1940	1950	1960
All functionaries (100:1900)							
Urban	100	122	186	296	432	590	860
Rural	100	118	164	209	390	735	790
Chancel functionaries (100:1900)							
Urban	100	122	167	270	341	430	575
Rural	100	143	187	254	298	485	560
Agency functionaries (100:1920)							
Urban	0	40	100	160	480	860	1,540
Rural	0	0	100	87	200	475	450

Table 18. Relationship of Chancel Functionaries to
Total Parishes, Catholic Population, and Secular
Priests, in Urban and Rural Dioceses

	1900	1910	1920	1930	1940	1950	1960
Parishes per functionary							
Urban	12.8	13.7	18.2	14.8	13.3	9.7	9.7
Rural	60.0	67.0	51.4	37.4	26.8	24.2	18.0
Population in thousands per functionary							
Urban	20.1	13.8	20.0	16.0	13.3	11.4	14.3
Rural	159.0	160.0	133.0	76.4	61.4	70.6	56.5
Secular priests per functionary							
Urban	17.2	18.3	20.0	17.5	16.4	11.7	11.7
Rural	95.0	114.0	91.5	69.7	53.0	59.5	45.0

Table 19. Change in Relationship of Chancel
Functionaries to Total Parishes, Catholic Population,
and Secular Priests, in Urban and Rural Dioceses

	1900	1910	1920	1930	1940	1950	1960
Parishes per functionary							
Urban	100	107	143	115	104	76	76
Rural	100	112	86	62	45	40	30
Population in thousands per functionary							
Urban	100	69	99	80	66	57	71
Rural	100	100	83	47	39	45	35
Secular priests per functionary							
Urban	100	106	117	102	96	68	68
Rural	100	120	97	73	56	63	47

Table 20. Relationship of Lay-Organization
Functionaries to Total Parishes, Catholic Population,
and Secular Priests, in Urban and Rural Dioceses*

	1900	1910	1920	1930	1940	1950	1960
Parishes per functionary							
Urban	0	1,040	431	338	102	63	35
Rural	0	0	360	433	23	12	13
Population in thousands per functionary							
Urban	0	2,500	1,120	835	284	192	135
Rural	0	0	397	468	23	13	20
Secular priests per functionary							
Urban	0	1,675	765	635	244	159	90
Rural	0	0	399	514	24	14	16

* For sources and definitions, see Table 15.

Table 21. National Catholic Welfare Conference;
Increase in Bureaus, Offices, and Departments, 1930–60

	1930	1940	1950	1960
Departments	6	6	6	7
Bureaus and offices	6	10	11	12
Total	12	16	17	19

Appendix C
NEEDS FOR FURTHER RESEARCH

The attempt to clarify the identities of the major faiths through their organizational developments sets the stage for some fundamental research. References were made to these needs and possibilities throughout the text. However, some summary comments on this problem may be useful. These suggestions are not developed as hypotheses but rather as areas for further exploration.

1. The character of Protestant organization needs to be clarified more fully through studies of presbyterial forms. The plans for the union of several major denominations may provide an occasion for this clarification. The research problem in the Protestant field is extremely serious because of the pluralistic structure and excessive cost of even modest sampling. For example, the Negro churches should be studied in considerable depth, especially as they emerge in the urban crisis.
2. Paul Harrison's initial study of power and authority should be followed in a representative sample of

Protestant organizations, and, in turn, systematically explored in Protestant, Catholic and Jewish organization. This calls for a careful investigation of the relationship between the power of the central staffs and the participatory power of the larger body, related to an appraisal of effectiveness in action over one or more events. There is some reason to think, from the present study, that these bodies are approaching a common pattern of centralized authority (on different principles) and pluralism of relatively autonomous, voluntary agencies. This may well be a distinctively American pattern of religious organization, combining authority and voluntaryism in a highly dynamic structure.

3. Relationships between managerial or line and staff personnel in the religious bureaucracies are much in need of investigation. Rankin's study in California opened up the fringes of this problem from the local side, but the internal problems of recruitment, advancement, distribution of power, and continuity are relatively unexamined.

4. The place of regionalism in the allocation of funds deserves careful study, since it represents a compromise between central authority and localism which may become the distinctive style of Protestant action. The controversy over realignment of regional authorities, to correspond to metropolitan developments, may well furnish an interesting focus for clarifying this problem.

5. The emergence of ecumenical instrumentalities for particular types of ministries and for joint action in the urban crisis deserves careful investigation. There seems to be far more common ground for action than might have been anticipated by the earlier history of these major faiths. This joint action may likewise establish certain common patterns of organization.

6. The Catholic organization on the American scene, and particularly the relationship between Boards and Bishops, deserves serious scrutiny from the inside. The dynamics of this new development in Catholi-

cism may be historic not only in the United States but for Catholicism throughout the world.

Costs are a crucial factor in contemplating such research needs. This study may help to reduce some of the costs by identifying central issues in organization.